Juggernaut over Holland

Juggernaut over Holland

THE DUTCH FOREIGN MINISTER'S
PERSONAL STORY OF THE INVASION
OF THE NETHERLANDS

BY EELCO NICOLAAS VAN KLEFFENS

NEW YORK
COLUMBIA UNIVERSITY PRESS
1941

Foreword

THE Dutch have a strange sympathy and liking for the under dog. Anyone who, rightly or wrongly, is a victim of superior force, can be sure of Dutch sympathy. The bad boy being taken to the police station can safely count on the crowd turning against the policeman. When Belgium and France suffered under the German invasion in 1914, the great bulk of public opinion in Holland was in favor of France and Belgium. But no sooner had the tide turned and Germany was found suffering under the exactions of the Versailles treaty and the occupation of the Rhineland and the Ruhr-district, than the Dutch felt great compassion for their Eastern neighbors. In recent times, the same characteristic found striking expression when the whole populace, led by the Government, spontaneously contributed large sums for the relief of Finland. The origin of this trait is perhaps to be found in the days when the Netherlands suffered from oppression, and there was engendered an aversion to all use of force against the weak. After Germany's collapse in 1918 the Dutch did a great deal to alleviate German suffering. The world has now had an opportunity of seeing how Germany reacted to the kindness and assistance Holland showed it in what Herr Hitler himself has described as

the darkest days of the German race. A few days after the
Nazis had invaded Holland, one of Holland's best-known
journalists in a broadcast to Germany referred to the aggression in the following terms:

"This has been done to us by those same young people
whom after the Great War we took unto ourselves in
Holland in order to protect them from hunger. Tens of
thousands of children came in relays to us: we gave them
milk, cheese and the best food we had, so that these German children, whom we regarded as innocent victims of
the war, should not fall victim to rickets or consumption,
should not get diseases which would mark them for life.
We sanctioned large loans, so that during the war and
after it food might be sent from Holland to German children. We took unto ourselves tens of thousands of small
boys, who got to know every inch of our land. The Dutch
were always friendly towards the Germans. That which
has befallen us is the work of our friends. Those children
grew up and assaulted with armed force a country which
they had become acquainted with when it had in its kindness given them food.

"What will happen to the name of Germany? Will
anyone ever again be able to act kindly towards Germans?
The name of Germany has become a synonym of con-
tempt, shame and daily increasing hate. And reasonable
Germans must realize that it is justly so. These German
children, grown up into men, have now murdered our
children, our wives, they have dishonored their own uni-

forms and ours which they have stolen. Is this the most soldierly nation in the world? Where is the honor of the German soldiers, of the German knights? Do not say that you have not killed civilians, women and children—I have seen it!

"I can no longer even hate you, I feel compassion for you, Germans. I am sorry for the German nation, that it endures such tyranny. You, Germans, are very sensitive to what the world thinks about you. Is it a matter of indifference to you what America thinks of you, the Vatican, every decent man in the world? Where is 'Deutsche Kultur' and 'Deutsche Treue'? What has happened to these conceptions? I know that many of you are falling victim to moral despair. But it is not yet too late. With what joy would the world see the German nation awake again to honor and reason. For there is no doubt as to the issue of the war. Even if you win battles now, you will lose the war. Why are you fighting? What will the war bring you? Deutsches Volk, erwache!"

Contents

Juggernaut over Holland

Introduction

UP TO that fateful Friday, the tenth of May, 1940, Holland was a well-governed country; a stable country; a country of steady progress where there was an exceptionally large measure of social justice; where wealth was more evenly distributed than in most European countries; where there was neither unlimited private wealth nor dire poverty; a country which wisely governed its overseas territories and had opened up their resources to all the world, while at the same time raising and striving further to increase the moral and material well-being of its native subjects; a country whose nationals had achieved distinction in the arts and sciences and had been awarded a disproportionately large number of Nobel prizes; where education was at a very high level; a constitutional monarchy which was known within and without its borders as a democracy; a country which coveted nothing belonging to anyone else; a land of liberty, of tolerance, and of patient, unspectacular labor and achievement.

Holland is one of the older and smaller states in Europe. Its eighty-year struggle against Spain, which came to an end in 1648, brought its emancipation—the rise of the Dutch Republic, as John Lothrop Motley called it. The half century that followed saw the consummation of its growth as a state; ever since 1715—the end, for the time being, of France's tendencies towards expansion in that period—the Netherlands has been a factor of stability in European politics, a role which, as contemporary history shows, by no means excludes a progressive spirit in internal administration. The Napoleonic era was a trial from which the Dutch again emerged free, thanks to their own energy, more united as a nation than ever before under the leadership of the House of Orange, in which from then on the crown of the Netherlands became hereditary.

In 1839 the unhappy union with Belgium, sealed by the Congress of Vienna in 1815, came to an end. Since then the Netherlands has stood somewhat aloof from the changing scene of European politics. The Dutch realized that their country's small size and population, its situation on the cross-roads of Western Europe at the mouth of the Rhine, the Meuse, and the Scheldt, made it essential for them (the policies of the surrounding great powers being what they were) not to become involved in alliances or understandings with any other power or group of powers. They perceived very clearly that neither France, Great Britain, nor Germany would tolerate the permanent influence over the Netherlands of any large state.

Successively, the governments of the Netherlands acted upon this conviction. Consistently, they followed a policy of no entanglements. At the same time, and although there were large sections in the country in favor of disarmament, they never fell into the error of disbanding their armed forces. They fully realized that measures for the defense of the country were indispensable if the dangers inherent in its becoming a military vacuum were to be avoided. This was their own interest but it was also the interest of the whole of Europe: the Netherlands should be firmly in the hands of the Dutch nation; it should never become too easy a prey for any unscrupulous invader; it should never offer a premium for aggression, either against itself or through it against other countries.

Holland lies at the intersection of lines of communication of world-wide importance and commands waterways of vital importance to all nations. This is equally true of the Dutch East Indies, Surinam, and Curaçao, the overseas possessions of the Netherlands. While under the control of a small nation like the Netherlands, such regions need give no anxiety to any country, provided the nation in control jealously guards its independence and does not enter into commitments with any big power or group of powers. This condition the Netherlands has always observed as scrupulously in the Dutch East Indies as in Europe. Dutch foreign policy thereby acquired a perfect singleness of purpose and of conduct, which gave it great strength, consistency, and a complete unity of action.

No alliances, no military conventions, no conversations with foreign general staffs could be entered into by the Netherlands. The country had no wish to participate even in such seemingly harmless contracts as nonaggression pacts. Herr Hitler found this out when in 1936 it suited his purpose to offer such a pact to Holland. The proposal was politely declined. This refusal did not spring from any opportunistic consideration, nor from any instinctive dislike and distrust of tyrants. The reason for the refusal was that the Netherlands considered one general treaty outlawing war—such as the Briand-Kellogg pact to which Germany was one of the parties—was enough, and that any new treaty to the same effect would necessarily have what might be called an inflationary tendency, a tendency to weaken, by multiplication, the authority of the previous treaty. Moreover, the Dutch believe that nonaggression treaties are not really necessary: they reason that either we live in decent international company—and then no nonaggression pact is necessary—or that we do not live in decent international company—and then a nonaggression pact is as futile as it is deceptive.

The Dutch have more faith in facts than in paper arrangements. Only in the case that a paper arrangement is an expression of some basic fact in the field of international politics do they have no particular objection to agreeing to it. When, in 1923, the Netherlands accepted declarations made individually by the United States of America, France, Great Britain, and Japan, to the effect that these powers undertook to observe the integrity of the Netherlands East Indies, it did so knowing that the integrity of the Netherlands East Indies is one of those basic needs in international politics: a political necessity of the first order. To accept an expression of this necessity on paper did not seem to the Netherlands to be a deviation from its tradition of founding a foreign policy as much as at all possible on hard facts and on nothing else.

But, it will be remarked, the Netherlands has in recent years adhered to the League of Nations, entering thereby into a political compact with a great many other states. This was not a deviation from its fundamental policy of no entanglements. Since they desire only to keep what is their own, the Dutch are partisans of an ordered international community. Anything seemed to them better than the anarchic community of nations as it existed before 1914. When, therefore, the League of Nations was founded with the main object of providing for the safety and integrity of member states and when (this, to the Netherlands, was a point of the greatest importance) this League promised to be universal in character, Holland decided to join it in order to help in giving the new organization a chance. Far from breaking with the country's well-established policy of no political collaboration with any specific power or group of powers, adherence to the League was no more than a new manifestation of that policy: the pursuit of the highest possible degree of security. Collective security was to take the place of "no entanglements." It was a change of methods, not of ends.

In Dutch opinion, the very universality of the League, as planned, was its saving grace. There would be no question of members being drawn into the orbit of any one particular power or group of powers. It can easily be imagined how great was the disappointment of the Netherlands when the United States failed to enter the League: this fact detracted from the character, attraction, and power of a universal League of Nations. But even so, the League seemed sufficiently general in its membership to make it possible for the Netherlands to join it, which was done very soon after the Covenant of the League came into force (1920). Everybody knows how short-lived were the hopes that were founded on the great institution of Geneva. The League's authority, if it ever existed, dwindled as the years went by. The abortive disarmament conference, the Manchurian affair, the Abyssinian war, the withdrawal of Germany, of Japan, and of Italy and all that followed took most of the League's precarious credit away.

When, in 1936, it was realized that the League of Nations was becoming increasingly powerless, and in particular that there was no longer any hope of general disarmament, the Netherlands played an active part in stating, together with the Scandinavian countries and Belgium, that it could no longer undertake to be bound by decisions of the League in matters of enforcing collective security. The League had failed, and it was for the smaller European powers an act of self-preservation to make this declaration. Thereby, without actually withdrawing from the League—what remained of this first attempt at international organization seemed worth keeping so long as there was nothing better—the Netherlands had returned to its original policy: no entanglements, coupled with a reasonable scale of national armament so as not to present any avoidable temptation to anyone to invade the country. Nevertheless Holland will always be in favor of any serious attempt to promote international coöperation, especially when this tends to give law and order a better place in international affairs than they have hitherto occupied.

It needs little reflection to realize that, in times of war, Dutch policy could only result in a tendency to maintain neutrality: it was this tendency which in fact manifested itself whenever a fresh crisis shook Europe. So it was in 1870, so it was also in the Great War of 1914–18. This suited not only the Netherlands; it also suited Europe, America, and Asia, and if ever there has been any merit in the foreign policy of Holland, it lies in the fact that its leaders have always succeeded in adapting the country's needs to those of the continents of which it forms part. As late as 1914, even Imperial Germany saw that it would be unwise to infringe upon the integrity of the Netherlands, knowing there could be no peace in Europe so long as the Netherlands was deprived of its ancient liberties. It was left for Herr Hitler to disregard this fundamental truth in European politics and it required his overbearing conception of Germany's ascendancy over all other powers to allow himself a step which for more than three centuries had been shown to be fatal.

The policy of neutrality pursued by the Netherlands in times of war between other states may be brought out into full relief by comparison with the neutrality of Belgium before 1914, or with the perpetual neutrality of Switzerland. Belgium before the Great War, and Switzerland since time immemorial, had been neutral because international conventions had prescribed it; the neutral status of these countries was defined by treaty. Dutch neutrality, on the other hand, was purely voluntary; the country was free to abandon it at any time at its own discretion. Belgian and Swiss neutrality was based on law—Dutch neutrality on policy. No other power could be absolutely sure that the Netherlands would not, at some given moment, abandon the traditional policy of neutrality and no entanglements. But the world had learned to trust to the wisdom and tranquillity of mind of the Dutch rulers, and these rulers have never forsaken the trust placed in their hands.

The reliability and the unadventurous character of Netherlands foreign policy made it possible for all powers to be on a friendly footing with the small Kingdom by the sea. Ties of friendship traditionally existed between the Netherlands and the great world powers, with Germany no less than with Britain and France, the United States and Japan. Not that the Dutch on the whole had a particular liking for the Germans. But they have long been used to dealings with all the nations of the earth, and there was little difficulty in finding a working basis for their intercourse with their Eastern neighbors. Because of common frontiers, trade and commercial relations between the two countries were considerable, thus bringing about close contact between Germans and Dutch. Many Germans settled in Holland. Large numbers of them merged with the native population, and after one or two generations were so completely absorbed by it that in outlook, in mentality, in behavior they could not be distinguished from people of pure Dutch descent. Others, however, associated themselves with the innumerable societies characteristic of German settlements abroad and remained completely German, so completely, in fact, that when Nazi pressure was brought to bear on them, they turned against the country which had given them a home and a livelihood.

There is one domain in the wide field of international relations which the Dutch made the object of their especial concern. It was the advancement of international law as a guiding and binding rule of intercourse between states. The Dutch, having no territorial claims on any other state, and having, as a seafaring and trading nation a major interest in a stable, well-ordered community of nations, have contributed as much as they could to furthering the rule of international law. The great work of Grotius, who wrote his immortal *De jure belli et pacis* during the second half of the eighty-year war against Spain, is too well known to require here more than a passing mention, and students of private international law know what such names as Voet, Huber, Bynkershoek, and others stand for. The close of the nineteenth century and the four decades of the twentieth saw a recrudescence of Dutch activity in this realm of thought. In 1899 and 1907, the two great Peace Conferences were held at The Hague, in the course of which the laws of war on land and at sea were codified, and rules were laid down for the pacific settlement of international disputes. As a result, the Permanent Court of Arbitration was established, and it was found a fitting tribute to the serene atmosphere of the Netherlands to make The Hague the seat of this international tribunal. American munificence provided the Court with suitable quarters and with a magnificent library by establishing the Palace of Peace, with its thousands of volumes on international law and kindred subjects. After the war of 1914–18, the Permanent Court of International Justice was established at the same place; its fruitful activities during nearly twenty years were interrupted by the events of September, 1939, but it may be hoped that once peace is restored to the world, a new era of highly important work will dawn for that institution. The Palace of Peace also housed The Hague Academy of International Law, where during the summer months professors and students from all over the world discussed subjects pertaining to the law of nations. New advances were made in the codification of private international law in the course of several conferences to which the Government of the Netherlands gave ready hospitality. The Hague had become the world's capital of international law, and, while it is fitting to acknowledge the contributions of all other states to this great work, it does not seem out of place here to recall that Holland sponsored it with all the means at her disposal for the common benefit of all nations that are of good will.

At the center of the dramatic scenes which we are now to witness stands The Hague. No doubt many readers of this book know that pleasant town, which a French author once aptly called the largest and most beautiful village in Europe. And indeed, a village it has always remained, in its curiously tranquil atmosphere. There is something leisurely about the behavior of its citizens. The unpretentious character of its simple houses, the comparative scarcity of large, striking buildings, its appearance of scrubbed cleanliness and its clear beauty all add to the impression of peace and happy living. The Hague is above all a center of governmental activity, the seat of Parliament, for which the Dutch have preserved the glorious old name of States-General. Here the Queen resides during part of the year in the unassuming Noordeinde Palace, a monument of Dutch simplicity of living and quiet dignity. Nearby, beyond a stretch of well-timbered parklike woods, lies the old "Huis ten Bosch," the "House in the Woods," where once lived William and Mary. Here, at the close of the seventeenth century, momentous decisions were taken which changed the map of Europe and exercised a decisive influence on the history of that continent; a Royal residence in the truest sense of the word, in spite of its small size. In the international sphere, the presence of the diplomatic corps lends color to Hague society life.

Around The Hague the fertile Dutch countryside unfolds itself, with its green meadows and bulb fields, its villages and towns, its broad rivers, broader estuaries, its innumerable waterways of every size, bathed in Holland's characteristic soft clear light under its mother-of-pearl skies. The serenity of the atmosphere harmonizes with the peace-loving nature of the inhabitants. Did not Frederick the Great say that the Dutch were essentially lovers of peace, and warriors only through necessity of circumstance? They are a nation of merchants and seamen, of hardy fishermen, a people advanced in agriculture and industry. Its scholars and universities have for centuries generously contributed to the common fund of human learning. Profoundly religious as a nation, they have always made tolerance one of their chief virtues.

In 1939, this happy nation had known exactly one hundred years of peace. A century before, the sad struggle with Belgium had come to an end, and no other war had afflicted the country since. Not that Holland knew no national problems. The economic world-crisis which began in 1929 had profoundly influenced the economic situation. There still was considerable unemployment; taxation weighed heavily. In the field of foreign politics however, the situation seemed satisfactory. There was no quarrel with any nation, great or small, and there seemed no particular reason to doubt further peaceful development.

Peace Island

IN Holland, the 31st of August has an importance all its
own: it is the Queen's birthday, a national holiday
for everyone. Flags fly from every house, Government
buildings are decorated and illuminated at night, the
streets and squares, where the bands play, are thronged
with happy, good-natured, jostling crowds. The foun-
tains in the beautiful Vijverberg in the center of The
Hague play in the sunshine—in the rays of the "Orange
sun"—which hardly ever fails to fulfil its promise of turning this day into a radiant festival for the whole nation.

Never had the Queen's birthday been celebrated with
more general and genuine joy than in 1938, when it co-
incided with the fortieth anniversary of her reign. It was
as if all her subjects wanted to pay their tribute to her
wisdom and restraint, to her deep understanding of the
country's needs which she, the longest reigning monarch
in the world, has always shown. The celebrations on the
31st of August, 1938, and the following days gave the
outside world a picture of a nation united in the common
love of its independence and its free institutions, in the
continuation of its ancient liberties of which the House
of Orange has always been the faithful and unselfish cus-
todian.

Striking was the contrast of the Queen's birthday in 1939 with the happy days of the year before. Instead of jubilation, political gloom cast its shadows on the festivities. Holiday spirit was quite lacking. The atmosphere seemed loaded with electricity. The people in this island of peace had the feeling of being surrounded by high-explosive material. Would the spark be struck which was to set the world around ablaze? The absence from their homes of so many husbands and sons who had been called to the colors and were now guarding the coast, the land frontiers, or vital points in the interior was enough in itself to take away all real gaiety from this saddest birthday the Queen had ever known.

During the last few days of August, 1939, Holland, together with all the world, was being swayed between hope and fear. That the Western democracies did not want war was everybody's firm conviction. That Germany did not want war was equally certain, with this all-important difference, that Germany's leaders were ready to go to extremes even if, thereby, war might prove unavoidable. Some of the German people backed their Fuehrer with fanaticism, some were terrorized into submission and silence, and a third category lived in a strange state of apathy. Yet it was certain that the nation would follow its Nazi masters wherever they might lead them.

On Friday evening, September 1st, we heard an important radio announcement from Berlin with regard to the strained relations between Germany and Poland. The

announcement was so worded that it seemed to justify
hopes that even such thorny questions as those of Danzig,
the Polish Corridor, and the treatment of minorities might
yet be settled by negotiation. Early next morning, however, these last hopes were dashed by the news that German troops had invaded Poland, and that the Polish army
was resisting. Once again, war seemed about to sow its
horrors over Europe. And indeed, next day brought the
news that first England and then France, in execution of
their guarantee to Poland, had declared that a state of
war existed between themselves and Germany.

In anticipation of this development, I had gone to my
office, that beautiful Sunday morning, at an early hour.
My faithful staff at the Ministry, all men of tried experience and devotion to the public cause, few in number but
unsurpassed in value, were there to carry out all measures
which had been prepared for some time past. Assuming
that in the beginning of the conflict at any rate, we were
not to be involved in it, we went for the last time over the
Proclamation of Neutrality which was to be issued immediately on learning that war had broken out. This document had been very carefully drafted by some of the best
legal minds of the country; in the event of war between
third powers, it was to define the status of the Netherlands, and to lay down regulations basing its neutral position on carefully stated rules of international law. The
Dutch have never adhered to the opinion that international law is too ill defined to serve as a basis for interna-

tional conduct. On the contrary, they have found that the rules of the law of nations can be stated with sufficient precision to be accepted by any government which is not bent on disregarding them. In the World War, the neutral status of the Netherlands had been based on international law and nothing else. In that difficult period, against the encroachments inspired by the interests of the belligerents, Holland had always fallen back on the dictates of law as the only impartial and objective means of ascertaining what her rights and her duties were, and what were those of the belligerents. We meant once again to follow this course of action by making law, and not some opportunistic conception, our guiding principle—and we did it.

Therefore, as soon as the news came of the outbreak of war, it needed little more than the pressing of a button for the Proclamation of Neutrality to be forthwith issued. This proclamation, addressed to all whom it might concern, began by stating that, in view of a state of war having arisen between a number of foreign powers, the Netherlands Government was resolved to observe complete neutrality, and then proceeded to enumerate in detail what that neutrality was to imply. These regulations have been scrupulously observed by the Netherlands Government; their contents, made known to all the world, have not been questioned by anyone as to their absolute conformity with accepted rules and principles of international law. Nor has any power, Germany not excepted, ever had justifiable reason to complain that these self-imposed

neutrality regulations were not impartially and fairly put
into effect. When Germany finally assaulted us, she felt
herself obliged to offer reasonings of an entirely different
order as justification for her outrage.

Parliament met almost at once. Both Houses fully en-
dorsed the policy of the Government, and thereby made
the meeting an impressive demonstration of national unity.
Rarely had the country been more at one than on that
occasion. This complete conformity of views with regard
to foreign policy between the Government and Parliament prevailed throughout the period of Holland's neutrality; only the small but vociferous group of our National Socialists provided an occasional jarring note.
When, in November, 1939, I had to defend the 1940
budget for the Ministry for Foreign Affairs in the Lower
House, the deputies cheered the declaration I made on
that occasion, and the representatives of all parties sealed
their adherence to the Government's line of action by
coming up to shake hands at the end of my speech. The
same took place when, two months later, I had to pilot the
budget through the Upper House. As in any sane democracy, there was criticism regarding this or that point of
Government policy, but in respect of the conduct of the
country's foreign affairs there was practically none.

Scarcely had war begun with the German onslaught
on Poland when our tribulations as a neutral state were
under way. In a war between great powers in the immediate vicinity, the position of a neutral state is far from

being an enviable one. That had been our experience in
1914–18; it was once more revealed to us in those last
months of 1939. Under such conditions, being neutral
makes little appeal to the imagination. There is nothing
romantic, let alone heroic, about it. Although maintaining
and, if need be, enforcing neutrality calls for coolness,
impartiality and courage, such a course is undramatic,
uninspiring and, in general, thankless; and yet neutrality
is the only possible course for a country in the geographical and political situation of the Netherlands. It cannot
enter into any alliance with any one great power or group
of powers without immediately bringing on its head the
wrath of some other great power, to which any such alliance must needs be anathema. For a country in the position of the Netherlands, any policy other than neutrality
would have been suicidal.

Once Germany had invaded Holland, voices in other
countries were not lacking to contend that if only Holland had entered into some defensive arrangement with
the Allies in time she would not have suffered the fate the
German attack brought upon her. This argument seems
altogether futile. There is not the slightest doubt that the
moment Germany had learned (and heaven knows her
intelligence service is ubiquitous) that the Dutch Government was plotting with the Allies she would have attacked at once, long before the Allies could have sent any
troops to our assistance. I must admit that, on the part of
responsible people in Britain, I have very rarely found any

lack of understanding on this point. No thoughtful person, taking into account all the facts of the situation, could reach any other conclusion.

On two occasions, once in November, 1939, and once in April, 1940, the Dutch Ministry for Foreign Affairs published a collection of documents—a so-called Orange Book—giving a survey of the principal matters dealt with by the Ministry in connection with the war which were suitable for publication. It is a pity that publications of this kind receive so little attention and real publicity. They are funds of information, and most illuminating to those who really wish to understand foreign affairs. But it seems to be their sad fate in all countries to pass unnoticed by the public at large, and to come chiefly into the hands of specialists who dissect them much as a dead body is dissected by the anatomist. Our Orange Books received no better welcome. And yet they give an excellent impression of the painstaking efforts of the Netherlands Foreign Ministry to keep the balance even between the belligerents, and steer the ship of state safely between the Scylla and Charybdis of the two opposing camps. These Orange Books constitute irrefutable evidence of the fact that the spirit animating Netherlands neutrality was one of unbiased impartiality, on the basis of international law. There has been no deviation from that path, whatever German propaganda may have endeavored to make the world believe after she had thrown off the mask and assaulted Holland. If anything, we were overscrupulous in affirming our will to be neutral, and so it was to the very last. On the fourth of May, 1940, less than a week before the German invasion began, the Minister at The Hague of one of the belligerent powers sent me a note with the request to be furnished with the silhouettes of our military aircraft and a few other details of the same order. Within an hour, he was in possession of my reply, in which I refused to give him any such information, although its military value, if any, could only have been slight. Principle had to come first. We could not entertain any suggestion of this kind, which subsequently might prove to be the thin end of the wedge to compromise neutrality.

The Netherlands Government—and I think I may say the whole nation—fully realized that so strict a policy of neutrality was far from presenting only advantages. If either of the two belligerent sides should disregard it and attack us swiftly, there could hardly be any question of concerted action with the other side, so that in any case assistance would be doubtful. But, as has already been pointed out, it was far too dangerous for a country in Holland's position to undertake even staff talks, to say nothing of pacts and conventions, with either of the belligerents; and since it was obvious that we could not enter into military arrangements with both parties at once, the only course left was to abide by our attitude of aloofness.

This necessarily rigid attitude gave rise to continuous trouble with both belligerent parties. In the World War it had not been otherwise, and those who remember the correspondence, often of an unpleasant nature, which was then exchanged between neutral powers (including the United States before its entry into the war) and the two contending sides, can easily realize how it was this time. The Orange Books issued by the Government furnish much material illustrating this point. A cartoonist of *Punch* was inspired to depict a small boy with a puzzled look asking his father if a neutral is a country both sides are at war with. There is a good deal of truth in this somewhat exaggerated picture of the joys of neutrality.

In the previous war, neutrality had one side which, through force of circumstance and not by any inherent rapacity, brought the neutral some gain. It will be recalled that many people in neutral countries made profits, ranging anywhere from modest to huge, by manufacturing and selling commodities the belligerents needed. This profitable side of the picture, unedifying though it may be, has been singularly absent in the early stages of the present war, for the belligerents had learned their lesson and through collective buying, and by fixing maximum prices and other means reduced the possibilities for would-be war profiteers. Thus, in the economic field, the fate of the smaller neutral in Europe became more unenviable than ever. Finding himself between the devil and the deep sea, he had to face huge expenditure in order to keep his armed forces on a war footing. Those who, like Norway, neglected this aspect of their neutral status, subsequently paid a heavy price for their easygoingness. World trade, as a consequence of the war, decreased in volume at an alarming rate, and it can be readily imagined what this meant for a seafaring country like Holland, whose adverse balance of trade had largely to be compensated by services rendered to other countries in the field of transport. While taxation increased to meet the Treasury's growing demands, the sources whence it had to come dried up like a spring in a droughty summer. Prices tended to rise sharply, the stock market fell, unemployment was rife: against less than 200,000 unemployed in the summer of 1939, there were 275,000 early in 1940, an increase which—even when due allowance is made for seasonal influences—is all the more remarkable when it is remembered that the mobilization of the army had absorbed a great number of unemployed. Unprofitable investment in war material prevented the formation of new capital which, in a country like the Netherlands with an ever-increasing population, is of vital importance. Such were the economic adversities of war for the smaller European neutral, a subject which might well have inspired a modern Duerer to do an etching of new apocalyptic visions to misery and ruin.

Why? was a question often asked those days. Why all this suffering, why this waste, why this halt in the nation's progress? Here was a country which had always earnestly endeavored to assist in improving international relations, in placing the international community on foundations of law and order, in short, in improving human intercourse the world over. Now it was made to suffer, even before the Germans invaded it overnight, through no fault of its own.

Why, indeed, do such afflictions beset an innocent country? It is a cry to which the human mind has no answer, it is the same cry that is raised in the presence of all human suffering which is, according to our standards, undeserved. Yet in spite of the difficulty of the situation in which Holland found itself placed, the whole country felt truly thankful for being spared the horrors of actual warfare. Thanks to the farsighted policy of the Minister for Economic Affairs, care had been taken that there should be considerable stocks of those overseas commodities which the country needed: there was enough to eat for everybody, enough petrol for transport, fuel for heating and industry, fodder for our livestock, fertilizers for our soil. In spite of the restrictions placed on shipping, the country's supplies of raw materials were satisfactory. Holland did as best it could, accepting the inevitable without complaining, thanks to a complete understanding of the situation. In spite of everything, and although the country was growing poorer at an alarming rate through war expenditure and all other adverse circumstances, the condition of the average citizen was, for the time being not unsatisfactory.

Many were the questions that arose between Holland and the belligerents during this period of its neutrality.

First of all, there were several cases in which the inviolability of Dutch territory or the air space above it was not respected by the belligerents. In every case which came to their knowledge the Dutch Government took appropriate action. They had the satisfaction, in many instances, of admission by the British and German Governments that mistakes had been made and that an apology was due. In other cases however, these Governments remained obdurate and it was all the more difficult to obtain satisfaction from them since they proved not to be prepared to accept a recourse to arbitration or other methods of impartial pacific settlement.

Many complaints were made concerning belligerent aircraft flying over our territory. The shortest distance between Britain and Germany leads across Dutch and Belgian territory; in making the shortest possible detour to avoid Holland and Belgium, belligerent aircraft nevertheless frequently flew over those two countries. It is difficult to say which of the two, Britain or Germany, was the worse offender. Suffice it to say that in many a case there was no evidence of intentional violation. The fact, however, of British planes having an apparent preference for nocturnal offenses whereas the Germans often came in broad daylight, flying at great altitude and hovering above Dutch territory, gave rise to the uncomfortable suspicion that what the Germans were really interested in was a thorough reconnaissance of our defenses from the air.

The Germans submitted to us several cases of British planes having flown over Dutch territory, of which we had no knowledge whatsoever, and which in many instances seemed to us pure inventions. The persistence with which such cases were submitted to us—based, as the Germans said, on their allegedly very superior acoustic instruments—gave us some misgivings. It seemed at times as if they were endeavoring to draft a brief against Holland for allowing such alleged violations.

Like other neutrals or nonbelligerents, the Dutch suffered damage, in addition to much annoyance, because of the Allied blockade. Germany's more sanguinary efforts to prevent supplies reaching Allied countries caused us great losses in ships and trade.

As soon as the war began, vessels on their way to Holland were taken to British control bases for examination. In the beginning, this examination of ships and cargoes took a very long time. Vessels were detained for days and weeks on end, with all the loss resulting therefrom to the interested parties even if in the end the ships and cargoes were released and allowed to proceed to Holland. Later on, the machinery dealing with such cases was improved, and worked with greater despatch. But even so it created a certain amount of ill feeling in Holland against the Allies, especially against Great Britain. This applies also to the extensive nature of the lists of commodities proclaimed by the Allies as contraband. The Dutch Government was obliged to enter into negotiations with the

Allies in order to reach some workable basis in order to obtain from overseas the goods the national economy stood in need of. The Allies saw that some concessions would have to be made to neutrals in order to prevent their economic life from being stifled, in spite of the fact that this implied that Germany would derive some benefits therefrom in the shape of exports to Germany from neutral countries. For these countries, especially those bordering on Germany, as do the Netherlands and Belgium, simply cannot live without considerable economic intercourse with the Reich. Negotiations to reach a settlement giving some mutual satisfaction lasted for months, and were only concluded a short time before the German invasion.

Germany's attitude regarding economic intercourse with the neutrals was a very curious one. She proclaimed the principle that the neutrals were to supply Germany with all they supplied in normal times. If they did so, Germany would raise no objections to their normal trade with the Allies. This clearly was a purely theoretical conception, devised to bring pressure to bear on the neutrals, for the duty thus held up before their eyes to keep up normal economic intercourse with Germany could only be fulfilled if that country, or the neutrals, or both, overcame the British Navy, which enforced the blockade of Germany. Finally, the Reich seemed to acquiesce tacitly in the result of the negotiations which had taken place between the neutrals and the Allies. Whether this was because Germany admitted that the result obtained was the best she could hope for, or whether the German leaders, having decided upon invading neutral countries, were no longer greatly interested in the matter, is a question to which Germany alone could give the answer.

From time to time, menacing articles appeared in the German press, addressed to the neutrals, for not taking stern enough measures against the restrictions placed on their shipping by the Allies. Criticism of this kind was as illogical as it was unjustified—for if Germany could not beat the Allied fleets, how could the smaller neutrals? But this fact did not seem to disturb the Germans in the least. It merely was part of the "war of nerves," which the Germans have made into a fine art, waging it on all the world. It is more than probable that they grossly overrated the effect of these tactics. In Holland, at any rate, we never allowed ourselves to be impressed with them, and never has this peculiar form of bullying made us deviate from what, as a sovereign state, we thought to be our true course.

The attempts Germany on her part made to prevent supplies from reaching the Allies, although far less effective than the British blockade of Germany and much less harmful to Dutch economic life as a whole, were particularly odious because they took considerable toll of human life. It had been anticipated that the Germans would try to make as much use of the submarine as they could. The previous war had made this obvious. But this

anticipation did not lessen the indignation felt in the
Netherlands when U-boats sank valuable ships of our
mercantile marine in cases which, according to accepted
rules of international law, afforded no justification for
such extreme measures. One instance adduced fresh evidence of the slight store the Germans set by international
conventions and of the brutality they do not shrink from
using in warfare. It was the sinking of the oil tanker *Slie-
drecht* in the open ocean no less than 150 miles west of
Ireland. The German submarine commander, having sunk
the vessel, left the crew to their fate in open boats on the
high seas in the stormy November season. Twenty-six
perished; only five of the crew succeeded after a full week
in reaching the coast of Scotland in a pitiful condition.
By the terms of the Protocol of London of April 24, 1930,
to which Germany still adhered, submarines may destroy
vessels only if adequate measures can be taken for the
safety of their crew. The German Government con-
tended that all requisite measures for that purpose had
been taken—the death-toll is an irrefutable witness to the
contrary.

Another similar case was the sinking of the Dutch vessel *Burgerdijk*, which was on its way from the United
States to Rotterdam with a cargo consigned in its entirety
to the Netherlands Government. It was sunk after the
submarine commander had stated that he was not even
interested in the ship's papers. Fortunately on this occasion no lives were lost, but the Government of Holland

asked for full reparation of the material damage and for punishment of the offending commander, reminding the Nazi Government that, in 1916, their Imperial predecessors had indemnified Holland in a similar case. But Nazi Germany is not Imperial Germany: the Dutch demands were ignored. No other course was open to the Germans, for they were determined not to make good their mistake and the case of the Dutch Government was unanswerable. In the end, however, it seemed to dawn on the Germans that destruction of neutral vessels by submarines cut into their own flesh. They knew full well that the Allies did not seize cargoes genuinely destined for neutral consumption, and realized that, the better neutral economic life was maintained, the more chances there were for Germany to derive some benefit from it. In the spring of 1940, therefore, feelers were put out by the German Government to find some means of reducing their alleged need to destroy neutral ships and cargoes, but it was too late: by that time so many U-boats had been sunk that for the time being they ceased to be a serious menace to neutral and Allied shipping.

Submarine warfare has been since the World War a traditional element in naval operations. A new element was introduced by the Germans in the use of the magnetic mine which, dropped into the sea from vessels or seaplanes, sinks to the bottom, rising to the surface through the magnetic influence of a vessel of sufficient size passing over it, and exploding against its keel. It was the sad fate of a large Dutch passenger steamer, the *Simon Bolivar*, to be the first victim of this new implement of war. At dawn, on a grey Sunday morning in November, a sudden explosion not far from a British lightship caused this vessel to sink rapidly. Hundreds of people, who the day before had left the shores of their homeland with the thought of taking up their work on the peaceful shores of the Caribbean Sea, suddenly found themselves struggling in the icy, oil-covered waters of the North Sea. Heart-rending scenes occurred. Parents were torn from their children, wives saw their husbands drown before their eyes. Their fear, their anguish, their lasting sorrow justify the question whether such weapons as the magnetic mine should be allowed in warfare, or whether they should be banned as was, in days of old, the poisoning of wells, and, in our own time, the use of gas. That question remaining unanswered for the time being, it was fortunate indeed that soon effective means were discovered to cope with this new menace at sea.

Considerable resentment was felt in Holland when German seaplanes started to machine-gun and bomb small craft navigating or fishing in the North Sea. No form of warfare is more cowardly: the bombers have nothing to fear in the way of retaliation as they are completely invulnerable against small, unarmed neutral craft carrying out their lawful pursuits. Nevertheless, when a Dutch newspaper of considerable standing took the liberty of calling such bombings gruesome, the German press retorted by saying that the German airmen had a "high code of honor," and that any criticism of their acts could not be tolerated. In order to be quite fair, mention should be made of the fact that in most cases, the bombing and machine-gunning of Dutch vessels by German planes in the North Sea took place by night, often not far from the British coast, and sometimes in the neighborhood of British convoys. Even so, care should have been taken to avoid making innocent victims, the more so as quite a number of cases of these cruel shootings of neutrals took place in broad daylight.

Despite the feeling aroused in Holland by these various German deeds, it should not for a moment be supposed that the Dutch condoned acts of the Allies which they considered unjust in point of law or of fact. Mention has already been made of the attitude taken by the Dutch Government towards certain aspects of the Allied blockade. Another point of considerable general interest in this connection is the reprisals taken by the Allied Governments when they had found that the Germans were laying mines without due warning. The Allies retaliated by announcing their decision, put into effect shortly afterwards, to intercept merchandise of German origin or belonging to German citizens in neutral vessels, even on the high seas. The Netherlands Government strongly protested against reprisals of this kind. They did not for a moment question the right of the Allies to take measures of retaliation when they had occasion to do so. But they held that the choice of reprisals should not be such that third parties, who were in no way responsible for the measures against which reprisals were to be taken, should be the victims of these measures no less than those against whom they were directed. The choice of measures of reprisal is large. Why choose a form of retaliation by which neutrals would be hit no less hard than the enemy? This simple statement of common sense was of no avail in preventing the Allies from carrying out their plan. They were too much absorbed in stopping German exports to drop the matter, even if it were prejudicial to the neutrals. Embarrassed as the Allied replies to the contentions of the Dutch Government sounded, they made it clear that neither France nor Great Britain was to be deflected from its purpose. Once more belligerent interest had silenced the voice of law.

All this will have made it clear that, although during the period of their neutrality the Netherlands was an island of peace amidst the turbulent currents of the European war, the path of the Government was not strewn with roses. Nor was the position of the nation in any way pleasant. Neutrality calls for considerable restraint in showing likes and dislikes for any one belligerent. In this respect, the Dutch press was admirable. Our newspapermen, always ready to assert the rights of the country and thereby lending invaluable help to the Government, showed that they had a clear understanding of the delicate position we held. This does not mean that newspapers as well as citizens did not have their sympathies; for when it is remembered how greatly the Dutch are attached to free institutions, it is easy to guess where the sympathy of the great majority of the population lay. Spiritual neutrality, whatever the Germans may vociferously claim to the contrary, is an impossibility. But in their public utterances, the Netherlands press was a model of self-control and impartiality which never degenerated into betraying its own convictions. The Germans, always on the alert to discover something that would give them the slightest pretext for claiming that the Netherlands had given up their neutrality and thereby justifying some German act of violence against them, had to admit, and in private conversation were ready to admit, that they had no grounds for complaint. Hence, in accordance with their habit of dropping their curtsey to justice and decency, they then tried to justify their attack on Holland by gross misrepresentations and pure inventions put forward as their list of grievances.

The Gathering Storm

AS the early months of 1939 passed by, a growing sense of uneasiness prevailed. Nazi Germany was on the march in Europe. It had already annexed Austria. Czecho-Slovakia had been divided and the Czechs subjugated. The Polish situation was becoming more and more strained, seriously affecting relations between Germany on the one hand and France and Britain on the other. What would be the end of this tense state of affairs? The Dutch Government viewed it with concern, despite a reasonable hope that Holland might not be drawn in.

The basis for this hope lay in the fact that soon after war broke out, Germany asked the Netherlands to protect her interests in Poland and in South Africa, including the mandated territory of Southwest Africa, one of the former German colonies. It seemed an excellent sign of Germany's intentions to leave Holland out of the war: could one suspect that, of all the countries she might have requested to take charge of her interests there, she would have singled out this country if her secret purpose was to wage war on it? At as late a date as March 27, 1940, Germany appeared to give us another token of her confidence by asking us to assume the protection of her interests in the Cameroons, an ex-German colony, now un-

der a mandate held by France. To the superficial observer,
this might well have been fresh evidence of a complete
absence on Germany's part of any aggressive designs
against our country. Yet we set no great store by it. We
knew too well that important decisions in Germany are
taken by very few people, if not by Herr Hitler alone;
all matters of routine are dealt with by bureaucrats who
know nothing of any momentous decisions which may
be under consideration, and those civil servants whose
business it is to look after German interests abroad belong
to this great majority, efficient in detail, uninformed in
matters of policy.

This guardianship of German interests cost many Dutch
diplomats and consuls a great deal of time and exertion.
To us, it meant no more than that; the only reward was
to be an assault on our country. None the less, at this time,
war seemed by no means certain. Would Germany, forcing the issue, challenge the united forces of Britain, France,
and Poland? Numerous thoughtful people in Holland, as
in America, doubted it. The prospect seemed too terrible,
and it is a common human weakness not to believe that a
disastrous development is inevitable until it is actually at
hand. Spring went on to early summer. Holland's tulips
bloomed as gloriously as they did in so many previous
peaceful years; the country had a look of quiet prosperity. What, except the columns of foreign news in the
newspapers, seemed to point to war?

It was in this atmosphere that, one day in June, my

wife and I set out for Berne. I had been designated some time before to take up the post of Her Majesty's Minister to Switzerland, where we were now proceeding in order to find a suitable residence in which to establish the Legation. We soon found what we had been looking for: a delightful house in its own grounds, in the outskirts of the quaint old Swiss capital. Life seemed very good indeed at that moment, with the prospect of an interesting post in a beautiful country which we were fond of and knew well, among a congenial population united with the Netherlands by a common love of free national institutions and by a friendship centuries old. Before returning to The Hague, we happily planned our future home and made all arrangements for its decoration and equipment, from carpets and curtains down to the champagne for our reception of the Dutch colony on the Queen's birthday on August 31st.

We planned to move in by the middle of August. It would be a welcome change, after many consecutive years in the Ministry for Foreign Affairs in The Hague.

But Fate had decided otherwise. By the end of July an unexpected Cabinet crisis arose. At the very moment when we were leaving our apartment at The Hague, the telephone rang. The Minister of State, who had been requested to form a new Government, wished to see me. I shall not forget that Sunday.

Jonkheer de Geer received me in his garden and with little introduction asked me to take the portfolio of Foreign Affairs in the new Cabinet. In spite of the honor, I felt very reluctant to accept. I had served in the foreign ministry for nearly twenty years and well knew what the burden of being at the head of that department implied. Some of its chiefs, able men, animated with the best of intentions, had reaped considerable public criticism for their toils. Others I had known had aged with undue rapidity under the strain. Still others, excellent civil servants, reaped little success in Parliament. Was I to give up my attractive Swiss projects for so hazardous a charge?

My doubts were not to last long. It was made abundantly clear that preferences would have to make way for duty. A week after saying goodbye to the Ministry for Foreign Affairs, I was back again as its head—not without courage, but filled with dark forebodings. Above Europe the clouds were rapidly gathering.

German relations with Poland, and therefore with France and Britain, were going from bad to worse. The new Dutch Government was at once filled with serious misgivings with regard to the trend of affairs in Europe. Foreign affairs loomed large in its daily preoccupations. Acting under the inspiring leadership of the Queen, the Government strove hard to leave nothing undone that might avert disaster. At the same time all measures were taken so as to be ready if the worst should happen. In Belgium, King Leopold and his Ministers were acting on similar lines. After consultation with the Dutch Government, the Government of Belgium took a first step, in the hope that this initiative might lead to a peaceful solution. It was expected at least to ease the tension so that friendly negotiations might be possible between the powers engaged in what seemed to have become a dispute of an acutely dangerous character. Realizing that a major armed conflict in Europe would gravely endanger the peaceful existence and the economic welfare of the smaller European states and guided by the wish to leave no stone unturned to preserve peace, the Government in Brussels issued invitations to those of Holland, Denmark, Finland, Luxemburg, Norway, and Sweden for a conference to be held in the Belgian capital, in order to discuss what might be done to influence the course of events. As a result, the Ministers for Foreign Affairs of those countries met in Brussels on August 23rd. Switzerland, too, would have been welcomed at the conference, but the Federal Council had let it be known that the scrupulous policy of perpetual neutrality resulting from Switzerland's international status prevented that country from taking part, in spite of its sympathy for the cause at stake.

There was something profoundly moving, even dramatic, about this gathering. The able Belgian Premier, M. Pierlot, and the Minister for Foreign Affairs, Mr. Spaak, a man of transparent honesty and steadfastness of purpose, acted as hosts. There was Mr. Munch, the Danish Foreign Minister, aged in the pursuit of a policy of almost complete disarmament, which he firmly believed to be the only one open to his country; Mr. Bech, for so many years at the head of the Grand Duchy of Luxemburg's foreign ministry; Mr. Koht, from Norway, his grave and somewhat ascetic mien recalling some character of one of Ibsen's dramas; the resourceful and energetic personality of Mr. Sandler, King Gustav's Minister for Foreign Affairs; the Finnish representative, tall, broad-shouldered Mr. Erkko, whose country then still seemed so safe and yet was to be engaged in a heroic struggle with the Bolshevik hordes before the year was out; and finally, myself. All these men had only one thought in mind: to do all in their power to prevent war from breaking out. They had the profound conviction that the result they sought to attain was the best that could be desired for Europe. Theirs was a voice crying and praying for peace. But at the same time their hearts were filled with fear, for the clouds darkening the horizon were blacker than ever. Inexorable fate against human hope and endeavor— tragedy seemed imminent.

It became clear to these men that ambitious schemes would be of no avail and were doomed to failure. The conference came to the conclusion that an urgent appeal, addressed by the King of the Belgians in his own name and in the name of the other heads of State represented at the conference, was all it could usefully propose. The text of this appeal was drawn up and submitted to the King's approval; that evening King Leopold, surrounded by the members of the conference, representing seven small peace-loving European nations, broadcast the following appeal from the royal palace in Brussels:

"Armies are gathering for a horrible struggle which will know neither victor nor vanquished. Public opinion in all countries is alarmed. That is why, in the name of His Majesty the King of Denmark, the President of the Republic of Finland, Her Royal Highness the Grand Duchess of Luxemburg, His Majesty the King of Norway, Her Majesty the Queen of Holland, and His Majesty the King of Sweden, and in my own name, each of us acting in agreement with his Government, I issue this appeal. We express the hope that the other heads of States will add their voices to ours in the same hope of peace and security for their peoples.

"The world is living in such a period of tension that there is a risk that all international coöperation should become impossible. The small countries are faced with the fear of a conflict into which they might be dragged in spite of their will to maintain their neutrality and their independence. Lack of confidence reigns everywhere. But there is no people which wants to send its children to their deaths. All the States have the same interest. Time is getting short. If we wait much longer it will become more difficult to make direct contacts.

"We want peace with respect for the rights of all nations. It is our wish that the differences between nations should be submitted to conciliation in a spirit of good will. Tomorrow hundreds of millions of people will be hoping that the differences which separate heads of States may be settled by means of conciliation. Let those in whose hands rests the destiny of the peoples apply themselves to settle peacefully the differences which separate them."

Early next morning those who had taken part in the conference hurriedly undertook the return journey to their respective capitals. It was an extraordinary departure: dense thunderclouds had settled like a pall over Brussels. Lightning streaked the skies in every direction; peal after peal of thunder burst upon our ears. The center of the storm seemed to be all around us in the very streets of the city; in less than no time a cloudburst had flooded its lower-lying parts. In this deluge, reminiscent of some ancient cataclysm, my secretary and I set forth by car for The Hague. At moments it became impossible to see more than fifty yards ahead. Fiercely the storm raged; it seemed a portent of what was to come a fortnight later.

Two days passed. The tension in Europe was increasing daily. On Saturday, August 26th, the German Minister asked whether I could receive him the same day; he had an urgent message from his Government to transmit. I saw him without delay, and this was the message he had been instructed to deliver:

"We are resolved to observe towards the Netherlands an attitude according to which, in conformity with the traditional friendly relations between the two countries and with due regard for the well-known Netherlands policy of independence, the inviolability and integrity of the Netherlands will in no circumstances be infringed upon, and Dutch territory will at all times be respected. On the other hand, we on our side expect, as a matter of course, that the Netherlands will, in case of an armed conflict, observe towards us an attitude of absolute neutrality. Above all other things, this implies that Holland, contrary to tolerating any infringement by third parties on her neutrality, would resist any such violation with all the means at her disposal. If, however, contrary to our expectations, the attitude of the Netherlands towards any such violation of her neutrality were to be different, it goes without saying that we should be obliged to safeguard our interests as dictated by the situation which then would have arisen."

On the face of it, this seemed a reassuring message with regard to the Netherlands. At the same time it implied very clearly that Germany, if not actually planning to provoke an armed conflict, was counting on one breaking out. On closer scrutiny, however, it could be seen to contain loopholes of the kind characteristic of Nazi diplomatic documents. What, in fact, would have to be considered as an "infringement by third parties on Holland's neutrality"? Would it be enough for Germany to assert that such an infringement had taken place, to justify her—even if to an impartial observer there were no infringement at all—in taking measures of violence against the Netherlands? Events later showed that the German subterfuge was even thinner than that. When Hitler was about to invade Holland, he did not allege that there had been an infringement of Holland's neutrality, but merely that he knew that some form of impinging on that neutrality was about to materialize, and that the Government of the Netherlands was aware of this.

It was clearly a case in which any question as to the real meaning of this ambiguous phraseology would have been left unanswered, unless some evasive answer were given. I therefore accepted the German Minister's statement without any questioning. He then proceeded to inform me that, in order to give these German assurances greater solemnity, he had been instructed to request that he should be allowed to repeat them to the Queen in person.

I could see only advantages in acceding to this request, in so far as that depended on me. If ever Germany, under some pretext or other, decided to violate our neutrality, this violation would be all the more serious if the alleged will to respect our position would have been solemnly pledged in the Queen's presence. I therefore at once asked whether Her Majesty was prepared to see Count von Zech. The reply being in the affirmative, the German Minister was received by Her Majesty in my presence. I remember those few minutes very clearly. Her Majesty sat motionless while the German diplomat once more read the text he had been instructed to convey. When he had finished, the Queen made no comment but merely said that she had taken cognizance of the message, and after engaging Count von Zech in conversation for a few minutes, brought the audience to an end. This interview left me full of uncomfortable forebodings.

Less than a week later, on the first of September, the British Minister handed me a declaration of a similar nature from his Government, in which the absence of circumlocution and qualifying terms made a happier impression:

"If in the event of a European war the Netherlands adopt an attitude of neutrality, His Majesty's Government will, in accordance with their traditional policy, be resolutely determined to respect this neutrality fully, provided that it is respected by other Powers."

France never made a declaration of that nature. This was a reason for the Dutch Nazis to take me severely to task in their daily paper for not having obtained such a statement. I decided not to reply lest I should do them too much honor. Two months later, however, when one of the few Nazi members of Parliament censured the Government, and me in particular, for the same reason, I reminded them of the fact that Belgium is situated between France and the Netherlands, and that therefore, since Belgium had obtained from France a promise of inviolability, the honorable member seemed to be victim to some strange confusion. Either this Nazi member believed in the value of France's assurance to Belgium and its corollary, that France would never undertake anything against Holland, or he had no faith in that promise. In the latter case, how could he attach any importance to a promise of the same kind made by the same power to Holland? This brought the discussion to a close.

When the appeal of the smaller European states, launched by the King of Belgium at Brussels on August 23rd, met with no response, Queen Wilhelmina and King Leopold, with the concurrence of their Governments, took a second step in order to leave nothing in their power undone which might possibly prevent an armed conflict from breaking out. Rapid consultations took place between Brussels and The Hague.

In the evening of August 28, the diplomatic representatives of Germany, France, Great Britain, Italy, and Poland were invited, in Brussels by my Belgian colleague, Mr. Spaak, and at The Hague by myself, to receive a communication. It was about midnight when I received the diplomats who had been summoned to the Foreign Office. I received them one by one, and told them that the Queen and the King of Belgium were prepared, if the powers to whom the communication was addressed should wish it, jointly to lend their good offices in order to effect a rapprochement between the prospective parties to a conflict.

Neither in Holland nor in Belgium did this offer receive any publicity at the time, so that initial discussions would not be hampered. The first press report concerning the offer came from abroad, where the initiative of the two Sovereigns met with little more than polite appreciation. If, alas, they were unable to prevent war from breaking out, there is no doubt that by making this offer the Queen and King Leopold did everything in their power to save peace. Their conscience and that of their ministers could be at rest.

While preparing to be ready for any emergency of war, we were determined at The Hague to leave nothing undone that could promote a return to peaceful conditions, and this determination naturally was stronger than ever when there was reason to reckon with an imminent danger for our own country. On Sunday, November 5th, I was granted an audience by the Queen, and placed before Her Majesty the idea of renewing to the belligerents the offer of good offices previously made in August, just before the outbreak of war. The Queen received the idea favorably, and arrangements were made at once to enlist the coöperation of the Belgians. As a result, King Leopold hastened to The Hague by car in the late evening of the following day, accompanied by Mr. Spaak. That same evening I made a first draft with my Belgian colleague of a new offer of good offices to the belligerents. The King remained at the Palace for the night, as did Mr. Spaak; their arrival had been observed by a journalist, so that it was widely known the next day and caused much speculation. A newspaperman questioned me as I left the Palace in the early hours of the morning, but of course I was not in a position to disclose anything as yet. Next morning, the draft we had made was discussed with, and, after some alterations had been made, signed by, the two sovereigns. In the afternoon it was sent simultaneously to the King of England, the President of the French Republic, and the Chancellor of the German Reich, each in their own language. The text of that document read as follows:

"At this hour of anxiety for the whole world, before the war breaks out in Western Europe in all its violence, we have the conviction that it is our duty once again to raise our voice.

"Some time ago the belligerent parties declared that they would not be unwilling to examine a reasonable and well-founded basis for an equitable peace.

"It seems to us that in the present circumstances it is difficult for them to come into contact in order to state their standpoints with greater precision and to bring them nearer to one another.

"As Sovereigns of two neutral States, having good relations with all their neighbors, we are ready to offer them our good offices.

"If this were agreeable to them we are disposed, by every means at our disposal that they might care to suggest to us and in a spirit of friendly understanding, to facilitate the ascertaining of the elements of an agreement to be arrived at.

"This, it seems to us, is the task we have to fulfil for the good of our people and in the interests of the whole world.

"We hope that our offer will be accepted, and that thus a first step will be taken toward the establishment of a durable peace."

When the news of this new offer of good offices had become known, the Kings of Denmark, Norway, and Sweden, as well as the President of Finland, at once signified their warm adhesion. Pope Pius XII telegraphed, giving his high spiritual authority to this joint plea for peace made by the monarchs of the Low Countries.

This was on Tuesday. A few days of anxious waiting followed. What would the answers be? Would the fact that the two Sovereigns of the Low Countries once more offered their assistance in bringing about a mutually acceptable settlement induce the Fuehrer to abandon such plans as we must assume he was entertaining for invading Belgium and the Netherlands? Such indications as we received regarding Germany's immediate military intentions remained very disquieting. Tension was in the air, and it was in that atmosphere that I had to defend the estimates for the coming year for the Ministry for Foreign Affairs. It gave me the occasion for publicly stating once again the firm determination of Holland to remain neutral. I made it clear at the same time that we would defend ourselves if attacked, so that nobody could count on an invasion being a military walk-over. Its favorable reception was a striking demonstration of the country's complete unity in its foreign policy and all its implications.

Very positive reports had by now come in to the effect that the German attack was to begin on Sunday morning, November 12th, at dawn. I assembled the heads of departments of the Foreign Ministry on Saturday afternoon, to discuss last measures with them. Every preparation had been made. Then, suddenly, messages began to come saying that something seemed to have changed in the plans of the German leaders. We looked at one another. Was the attack to be abandoned after all? After another hour of doubt and uncertainty, I left my office for home, where, at 5.30, the German Minister asked if he could see me at once. His face, as he came in, wore, if anything, an expression of relief. He showed me a telegram. It merely said that the renewed offer of good offices was receiving the earnest consideration of the German Government.

The tension was broken; the attack, if not abandoned, seemed at least to have been postponed. The dreaded Sunday morning dawned, but brought no invasion. What it did bring, were the answers from the King of Great Britain and the President of France. Both referred to previous public declarations of their statesmen in which the essential conditions for peace, so the telegrams said, had been sufficiently explained. Both gave to understand that it was for Germany to make known whether she was prepared to enter into those views. The British reply ended by saying that if the Sovereigns of the Low Countries were able to communicate any proposal from Germany of such a character as to afford real prospects of meeting the Allied desires, the Governments of the British Empire would give them their most earnest consideration.

The German reply, which came four days later, and was conveyed orally by Herr von Ribbentrop to the diplomatic representatives of Holland and Belgium in Berlin, declared on behalf of the Chancellor that "after the brusque refusal of the offer of good offices by the French and British Governments, the German Government considered this offer as having lost its object."

Since there had been no question of any brusque refusal by President Lebrun or King George, it was clear that the Germans would have nothing to do with the proposal. This was stressed by the unusual form in which the German reply came. Hitler had spoken on October 6th, the door he had then opened almost imperceptibly had been closed again when nobody showed any desire to enter. Overtures by the Fuehrer are made once only. The prestige of a dictator seems to make this unavoidable. That, probably, is the reason why nothing came of the second offer of good offices. But even if it had only had the effect of postponing the attack on Holland planned for November 12th, it served a good purpose; for the defenses of Holland and Belgium were far less strong in the autumn than they were to be in May, 1940.

The November crisis was by no means the only one in the period of Holland's neutrality. Another serious alarm was given in January, 1940; this time it came from Belgium. There, a German military plane, manned by two officers, had made a forced landing near the frontier. Immediately upon landing, they endeavored to destroy a bunch of papers they had with them. Their attempt was frustrated by Belgian soldiers, who took the documents into their custody. The Belgians showed considerable alarm. Strangely enough, the exact contents of these documents were known only to the King and a few of his most intimate military advisers. Whatever these contents were, the fact remained that all military precautions in Belgium were being taken once more with the greatest energy. A chief of the Army Staff was removed and another general put into his place; steps were taken to increase the powers of the military authorities.

This action by our southern neighbors puzzled us. We, on our side, had no indication that there was any imminent danger. The season seemed at its most unfavorable for any large-scale military operations. A long spell of frost, which had begun in December, still confined the country in its icy bounds and was particularly severe in Germany, where communications had become difficult. In addition to this, our Intelligence Service did not understand why the Belgians were so alarmed. Nevertheless, we decided to increase our vigilance to some extent in order to risk no chance of a surprise attack, but we left it at that. Nothing happened, and comparative quiet set in again.

Life at The Hague was fairly normal in those days. If

it had not been for the ubiquitous military uniforms and the khaki knitting seen lying about in homes everywhere, there was little to remind one that a war was in progress. Some curious situations, however, arose in the social field, since it was naturally impossible to entertain German and Allied diplomats at the same time. Great care had to be taken when issuing invitations. When my wife and I held our New Year's reception—a traditional function for the Foreign Minister at The Hague—matters were so arranged that the Germans came during the first hour, and the Allied representatives during the second.

With the advent of spring, days grew longer, and the weather improved. Hitler's armies had scarcely moved during the long and exceptionally cold winter months. Could he be expected to play the waiting game forever? Experts in all countries agreed that Germany was not in a position to endure a long war. For her it was a matter of swift success, if she were to have a chance of winning. As the season grew more appropriate for active warfare, the chances of a violent campaign breaking out increased, and the dangers for the neutrals thereby became daily more acute.

Ominous signs were not lacking. Even before the invasion of Denmark and Norway (Sweden escaping only by the grace of Russia), the Dutch police arrested numerous German spies. Why should there be so much spying going on in the country, if the Germans had no evil intentions towards it? Strange things were observed. The rear windows of the German school at The Hague had been pasted up with paper, but when the police searched it they discovered nothing. Since the outbreak of war there had been an abnormal increase in the staff of the German Legation, an increase far greater than that of the staff of any Allied Legation. What was the task allotted to all those Secretaries and clerks? One evening, the police were handed a large envelope. It was addressed to an office of the Nazi party in Berlin, and was obviously destined to be taken by messenger across the German frontier where it was to have been posted. Some careless person had lost it. The parcel was found near one of the buildings used by the German Legation. Since there was no sign of its having any diplomatic character, and as the address and the mode of transmission gave rise to suspicion, it was opened. The contents were amazing: they clearly proved that a man who had been an Attaché to the Legation for several years was the head of German military espionage in Holland. He appeared to have under him another man, whose identity was never revealed but who worked under the name of Jonathan, whose task it was to coördinate the data supplied to him by a number of spies, each of whom had a serial number corresponding to the same number given to some district of the Netherlands in which he was to operate. These spies obviously had been carefully trained and instructed, although it was clear that they were not all military men.

They described, in incredible detail, all they were able to discover in connection with the defense of Holland. They made surveys of fortified positions, inundations, trenches, cantonments, bunkers, in short everything that they could get any information about. They reported conversations overheard between young officers in some well-known restaurant. They talked with their landladies, their servants, or members of their families. These papers constituted an invaluable find for the Dutch authorities, and enabled them to round up a number of these spies, some of whom stated when tried that they had been terrorized in various ways into doing espionage work.

At the same time, however, this went to prove beyond doubt, that Germany was interested in our defenses to an extent which gave rise to the gravest misgivings. A complete list of the discoveries in this connection which were made in Holland, and against which immediate measures were taken with all possible despatch and energy, would be too long and too monotonous, moreover, to give here. The ultimate effect was for the Dutch Government to take an extreme measure of precaution. Towards the end of April, martial law was declared for the whole country. This gave the Government, and especially the military authorities, considerable powers, the exercise of which would normally have been against the Constitution. In order to track all subversive espionage, censorship on communications by mail, telephone, and

telegraph was imposed. The right to hold public gather-
ings and of habeas corpus were curtailed and other similar
measures were enforced.

The military authorities were being kept constantly informed, in so far as they were not already informed
through sources of their own. Although prospects looked
very dark, we never for a moment thought of revealing
what we knew to the Allies; experience goes to show that
any rash communications of such a nature, made to third
parties, always become known, and if that happened, the
Germans would undoubtedly have charged us with a
breach of neutrality. We would merely have played into
their hands by any such imprudent action, the more so
since it was doubtful what help the Allies could give us,
especially at such short notice.

The Dutch diplomatic missions abroad, as well as our
Intelligence Service, did their utmost to inform the Government as fully and as rapidly as lay in their power. What
they reported was always interesting, sometimes more or
less alarming, but never so far—except in the critical days
of November, 1939—positive in announcing an imminent
menace to the country's safety. On Saturday, the 4th of
May, however, we quite unexpectedly obtained information to the effect that an invasion of the Netherlands
might have to be reckoned with within the next few days.

This report, without giving certainty with regard to
the date on which the attack was to be carried out, seemed
very positive and came from a very reliable source. We

passed it on to be checked by other agents; next day, confirmation was received from another quarter, although equally indefinite about the exact date of the projected attack.

The German propaganda services of Dr. Goebbels in those days were trying to focus all attention on the telephone conversation which they alleged had taken place between the British Prime Minister, Mr. Chamberlain, and the head of the French Cabinet, M. Paul Reynaud, and according to which plans had been made in order to extend the theater of war by the 20th of May to southeastern Europe and the regions of the Mediterranean. On May the 9th—one day before Holland, Belgium and Luxemburg were invaded—the German press especially stressed the declarations made by Lord Halifax in the House of Lords concerning the reason why British troops had then been withdrawn from Norway, in the course of which he stated that this withdrawal had been decided upon in order to begin fresh operations elsewhere. This the Germans coupled with a remark made, so they said, by Mr. Duff Cooper, the British Minister of Information, from which they concluded that the Allies were again out to catch small neutral states in their nets, this time in the Balkans. It is worthy of note that the Netherlands and Belgium were not mentioned, which did not prevent the German papers from proclaiming the next day that according to their knowledge the Allies had been contemplating for a long time an attack on Germany through Belgium and the Netherlands. Lack of logic and consistency have never troubled German propaganda much.

If there were any need for confirmation that diversion of attention was the aim of the German Government, the radio of the Reich provided all evidence that could possibly be required. Very striking was the completeness with which this feint was supported by Italy. Collaboration by the Italian radio extended even to those items which at the very last moment purported to reassure the Low Countries. Most active of all the axis stations, however, were the German transmitters. To give a specimen of the tricks used to divert attention from Germany's true aims, a broadcast made by the Deutschlandsender of May the 8th—two days before the invasion—taken at random, may be reported here:

"The revelation of British plans in southeast Europe has created such an impression on the respective nations that England's warmongers now resort to employing an equally dull and clumsy manoeuvre to divert their attention. To this effect they use American press agencies which spread the news that Holland is gravely threatened. It is the old method—'Catch the thief'—which is being employed here. Thus Associated Press reports having learned, from a highly reliable source, that two German armies were advancing on Holland from Bremen and Duesseldorf at such a speed that they would reach the frontiers shortly.

"We are in a position to state that the reliable source of this military nonsense is the British Ministry of Information. This British Ministry of Information has been so hard hit by the German revelations of the imminent Anglo-French intentions that a manoeuvre to distract attention has to be staged willy-nilly."

Dr. Goebbels has always excelled in finding scapegoats. For a long time, the Jews were the chief culprits. Thereafter the British Secret Service, the "international bankers," or the oil companies were guilty of everything. This time the British Ministry of Information was to blame.

The Netherlands Government never for a moment allowed themselves to be lulled into a feeling of security by such manoeuvres. Our sources of information, which we knew to be reliable, continued sending news of an alarming nature. Absolute certainty there was not; but then, Germany being what it is, under a highly centralized leadership, absolute certainty could hardly be expected. By putting two and two together, however, a composite picture was obtained which was enough to cause the most serious alarm. Even then, the Government did not warn the Allies: we wanted to be absolutely certain that a founded accusation could never be made against us for having secretly abandoned the neutrality we had so consistently observed. All we did, by way of precaution, in the direction of London and Paris, was to send sealed orders by courier to the heads of the Dutch Legations in those capitals, the contents of which were in no way in-

dicated to them, and which they were only to open on
the receipt of a given code word.

It is a very curious fact that, in the course of the days
immediately preceding the attack, the German military
and air attachés at The Hague stated time and again that
the military authorities in Berlin were unable to understand why the Netherlands Government was taking such
extensive measures. Did they really know nothing? With
the centralized leadership as it exists in Germany today,
that is possible: subordinates are not informed until the
last minute. Or was it deceit? Perhaps we shall never
know.

On Wednesday, May the 8th, rumors were current in
German circles in Berlin that the British Navy was preparing a landing on the Dutch coast. Since we had not
the slightest indication to that effect, our Military Attaché
in Berlin saw the head of a department in the German
Army High Command who acted as liaison officer with
the foreign military attachés in Berlin, and told him that
the Netherlands Government had no reason whatsoever
to be apprehensive of a British landing. Nevertheless, he
added, all measures had been taken, both by sea and on
land, to counteract any attempt at landing by armed
force, adding that the Netherlands were perfectly able
to maintain their neutrality themselves and that they were
in no need of "protection" from any quarter. The German colonel replied that he quite understood this attitude, which he said fell completely into line with the

strict neutrality which the Netherlands had constantly observed. It is interesting to compare this declaration with the accusations of unneutrality which poured forth from the German Propaganda Ministry two days later, after the onslaught had begun.

As the storm relentlessly gathered force, all the measures, taken with great energy by the Dutch Government in close collaboration with all loyal citizens, were to be of no avail. The straightforward, impartial policy of neutrality which Holland had so rigidly observed, the efforts made to increase military preparedness, the struggle against espionage and subversive action—it was all to be in vain. Fate as interpreted by Germany had decreed otherwise.

The Venlo Incident

IN November, 1939, occurred an incident which
gravely preoccupied the Dutch Government. Germany's strange attitude, after the occurrence, is hard to
explain if there were no ulterior motive behind it. The incident, which received considerable attention in the press,
was as follows. In the middle of October the Chief of the
Intelligence Service of our General Staff was told by a
Major Stevens that British agents were in touch with a
group of high officials in the German army. Major Stevens
was a Secretary of the British Legation at The Hague, as
well as chief of the British Passport Control Office. We
had some reason to suspect that he was also engaged in
intelligence work for his country. After this startling
piece of information, Major Stevens added confidentially
that he had received instructions from London to enter
into discussions with these officers with a view to ascertaining whether a basis could be found for possible peace-
negotiations. In corroboration of what he said Major
Stevens showed his instructions to the Dutch general on
whom he had called. Since, he said, it was impossible to
conduct these discussions in Germany or in England, the
parties were anxious to have them held on neutral territory, preferably not too far from the German frontier,

and he added that, in addition to himself, an officer by the name of Captain Payne-Best, a British resident of long standing at The Hague and married to a Dutchwoman, had been appointed to take part in the discussions. He requested that measures should be taken to prevent the aliens concerned from being taken into custody by the Dutch police or military authorities when meeting in the frontier zone, where foreigners were limited in their movements.

The head of our Intelligence Service saw no reason to withhold his permission. But in view of the fact that the discussions were to take place on Dutch soil, he considered that he should be acquainted with what was to take place. For that reason, he instructed a member of his staff to attend the meetings. This officer, Lieutenant Klop, was to see to it that the talks should not degenerate into any violation of Holland's neutrality. In so far as is known to the Dutch authorities, two meetings took place in two different localities. On the 9th of November, there was to be a third one near Venlo, a provincial town in southeastern Holland, a few miles only from the German border. Major Stevens and Captain Payne-Best, accompanied by Lieutenant Klop, arrived there in a car driven by a Dutch chauffeur. The party proceeded to a café in the immediate neighborhood of the frontier, a few yards from the imaginary line separating Holland and Germany, and beyond the last Dutch military outpost. The moment the car stopped, its occupants were fired upon by a group of men who had jumped from a car waiting just across the boundary line, had dashed across the line and opened fire. One of the party, probably Lieutenant Klop, appears, according to what eyewitnesses there were, to have been killed outright; his body, together with his three companions, was dragged by the assailants onto German soil. The whole incident was over in so short a time that the Dutch frontier guards, although they were only a short distance away, could not get there in time to prevent it.

The men who had made this attack were civilians. There could, therefore, be no reason for the Government of the Netherlands to hold the German Government responsible for the application of such gangster methods on Dutch territory. So the German Government was merely requested to investigate the matter, as the kidnapers had taken refuge in Germany. It can easily be surmised how painfully public opinion in Holland was surprised when, shortly afterwards, a German press communiqué stated that the attack had been perpetrated by German agents. Immediately, the Dutch Government voiced their most serious objections and asked for an explanation. The German attitude thereupon became very strange: no reply was ever given to the Netherlands Government, in spite of the gravity of the offense and their repeated demands for an explanation. The impression was obtained that neither the German Legation at The Hague, nor even the German Foreign Office in Berlin really knew what was behind it all: the Gestapo once more had exercised its prerogative of being a law unto itself.

As the German Government persisted in refusing to furnish an explanation of this gross violation of the territory of a friendly power by its agents, the Netherlands Government instructed its Minister in Berlin to inform Herr von Ribbentrop that it was impossible for the Dutch Government to acquiesce in such an unsatisfactory state of affairs, and that they therefore made a formal proposal of submitting the Venlo incident to some impartial body to be designated by common consent. This body should be either a special German-Netherlands commission, or the Permanent Commission of Conciliation which still existed between both countries by virtue of a fifteen-year old treaty. If neither of these agencies was acceptable, we proposed a board of arbitration, or some international judicial agency. The choice was left entirely to the German Government, and it is difficult to see how the Dutch Government could have adopted a more liberal attitude, while showing clearly at the same time that they were out to vindicate their rights and to have the truth established. This offer, too, was of no avail. Never has the German Government made any reply, until, on the very day of the invasion, it was revealed why this silence had been so scrupulously maintained. At the moment of the invasion, the Venlo incident was inflated by Herr Hitler into some monstrous collusion of his own invention between the Netherlands and the Allies. Yet the Germans apparently had found it so little dangerous or objection-able that they had completely ignored it from November, 1939, until May, 1940. They had in fact been carefully preserving it to be used, in the absence of any authentic grievances, as the stick with which to beat the dog. It may be that Nazi zealots set store by such tales, as dis-torted out of all proportion by the "Ministry for the En-lightenment of the People and for Propaganda." Few others, forewarned by countless instances of German manipulations of truth can have been deceived. The chief interest of the abuse made of the Venlo incident lies in its value as an example of the technique of Nazi propaganda. Six months after the incident had occurred, it was dragged out to justify Germany's aggression against Holland. Nazi propaganda usually grasps some actual fact, and then pro-ceeds to twist, distort, exaggerate, or minimize its sig-nificance, with an eye to the goal to be attained, posing the while as the only true interpreter of happenings which the Jews, the British, the plutocrats, the "international bankers," or other scape-goats used by Dr. Goebbels have been trying by some low cunning to conceal from the world.

To Arms for Defense

AS THE Netherlands Government became more and more convinced that the calamity of war between the great powers of Europe was imminent, it took measures accordingly. As tension grew, and even before the 20th of August, measures of a military order were gradually taken to put the defenses of the country in a state of readiness.

Like so many other democratic nations, Holland had been economizing on her defenses. Instead of using money for armaments, she had used it to improve the social status of her industrial workers and peasants, to develop her educational system, to build bridges and roads. Steps had now to be taken rapidly to try to make up for arrears which had been accumulating in the field of military preparedness. But the armament industry of the country possessed a very limited capacity. We were forced, given the rate and extent of our rearmament, to place many orders for arms and munitions abroad. This was done in many countries: the United States, Sweden, Switzerland, Italy, France, Hungary, and also in Germany.

Germany had agreed to supply us with antiaircraft guns and some other war material, but only on the condition that part of the payment was to be made in advance. Since we could not obtain all we wanted on less onerous terms, the only course left was to accede to that demand. But after one or two guns had been delivered, no more were forthcoming. We claimed, we protested, we tried to investigate where the source of the trouble lay. On careful inquiry we found that it was not the economic authorities who were making difficulties; even the army bureaus had no objections. The man who was stopping the deliveries was Herr von Ribbentrop. As may be imagined, this circumstance was not at all to our liking, for although Hitler is reputed to make all vital decisions by himself, my German colleague is commonly supposed to be one of those who have found favor in his master's eyes. He is supposed to be "in the know" about some of the more important secrets. If, therefore, Herr von Ribbentrop was out to prevent war supplies from reaching Holland, he either knew of plans already decided upon against us by his Fuehrer, or he believed that Herr Hitler was engaged in evolving some such plan. Of course there was the possibility of its all being "Nervenkrieg"—fortunately, we were by now used to facing such situations coolly. We continued trying to get as much information as possible and to act according to our lights with the knowledge that in this world one cannot be aware in every issue, however important, of all the relevant factors.

Various quarters had expressed doubt as to whether the Dutch would fight, if attacked. Such doubts have always been strongly resented in Holland and events have shown how utterly unfounded they were. The Netherlands have at all times been ready to defend their liberties. Although they detest any glorification of militarism as it is to be found in the writings of German philosophers like Clausewitz and Treitschke, they are well aware of the fact that no nation deserves its liberty which is not prepared to defend it. They also know that, even if military resistance is temporarily overcome, it holds the promise of national resurrection at a later date.

The Dutch are not naturally inclined to give much time or money to military preparations. When they feel that they must fight, they are better soldiers than those of many another nation. But they dislike all that is disciplinarian, and their heart is not in routine drill, mock fights or manoeuvres, however necessary they know them to be. As a result, there is a perpetual tendency to pay too little attention to the requirements of national defense, social welfare and education being regarded as more congenial objects of expenditure.

After the war of 1914–18, considerable economies had been effected at the expense of military preparedness. The belief that the League of Nations would inaugurate a long spell of peace was the justification. But when it became apparent that the advent of the Third Reich meant war, measures were taken, although not nearly on as vast a scale as circumstances really required, to make up for arrears.

When by the end of September the Polish campaign

came to an end and Herr Hitler transferred the bulk of his troops to the West, a situation soon developed which clearly showed that these military preparations should be pressed forward with all possible energy. Early in November our Intelligence Service received reliable information to the effect that the Germans contemplated an early attack on the Low Countries: on Belgium as well as on Holland. These reports were soon borne out by various kinds of circumstantial evidence. The situation had to be regarded as decidedly serious. Of course there was always a chance that the Germans were trying, in a particularly intense degree, their methods of "Nervenkrieg." It was not only the fact that the Germans were massing troops and material along our southeast frontier which alarmed us, although the array of their preparations was impressive enough. Munition dumps had been established in the immediate vicinity of our territory, innumerable pontoons were lying in readiness to assist attempts at crossing rivers, airdromes were being laid out in the same neighborhood in great haste. An additional disquieting factor was the discovery that all kinds of Dutch uniforms, belonging to the Army, the police, postmen and railway conductors, were being smuggled into Germany. What did the Germans want these uniforms for unless it were in order to use them as camouflage in an attack? This smuggling of uniforms, far from being a mere rumor, is a well-established fact. Several arrests were made on the strength of irrefutable evidence.

The military authorities tried to speed up their preparations as much as they could, although at that time, scarcely two months after the war had started, the work was not nearly completed. At the same time those responsible for conducting the Kingdom's foreign policy did their best, as they had always done, to prevent the armed conflict from spreading. On October 6th, at the end of the Polish campaign, Herr Hitler had made his well-known speech in Berlin. Although this speech was far from clear, it adumbrated the establishment of a Polish State, be it only after amputations. It did not give the impression of excluding an autonomous Czech State. Its chief defect seemed to be that it pointed towards an intention on the part of the Germans to gain effective and exclusive domination over all the peoples of Central Europe. But it seemed to me worth-while that Germany's exact terms should, if possible, be ascertained. It still is my firm conviction that Herr Hitler meant his speech to convey his readiness to enter into negotiations for peace and that this peace could have been had on terms which at least deserved consideration. The very same evening the speech was made, I thought it my duty to ascertain, through a suitable private intermediary, whether there was any readiness on the part of the Allies to examine such possibilities as there might be. It must be admitted that Hitler did not make it easy for any outsider to understand that he really might be ready to compromise. In any case, I received no encouragement, and it all came to nothing without having even been attempted. In the light of subsequent events this seems greatly to be deplored. When war actually broke out in September, the progress of Dutch military preparedness was by no means inconsiderable. Much, however, was still left to be accomplished, in the field of equipment and training as well as in that of building lines of defense on modern principles.

The invasion of Norway taught our military authorities a number of lessons. From the manner in which that unfortunate country had been so rapidly subdued, the chief conclusion was that it was imperatively necessary for us to take some effective action against the possibility of the Germans landing considerable numbers of troops from aircraft coming down either on airdromes or on broad motor roads. Holland possesses mile after mile of broad, concrete roads, on which, provided only there is not too much wind, such landings may readily be effected. For long distances there are no trees or other impediments to make this impossible. A complete plan had therefore been worked out to frustrate any such attempts. Tall steel plates were to be erected in the middle of these roads in the direction of their axis, at given distances; these plates were available in sufficient numbers, so that this plan could have been carried out in three weeks along the roads we feared the Germans might use. When, however, the news came that we had seriously to count on the possibility of an immediate attack, emergency measures were taken. Instead of using steel plates, we tried a more expeditious method: part of the roads were obstructed by any kind of obstacle—old lorries, old buses and other material suitable for the purpose. Traffic on these roads became, of course, somewhat hampered, but this seemed more than justifiable. Events were to show that this emergency measure, coupled with the placing of various kinds of obstacles on airdromes, reducing the size of some and making others unfit for use, meant a great disadvantage to the Germans and seriously upset their calculations. Instead of reducing Holland to impotence in one day, on which it was proved later they had firmly counted, they had to fight hard for five days in order to overcome in the greater part of the country the stubborn resistance of the Dutch land forces.

Vigilance had reaped one of its rewards. Whatever margin the German General Staff may have allowed for errors of judgment and possible setbacks, it goes without saying that the execution of a plan designed to be carried out with clockwork precision must be seriously impaired if some important part of the project requires a period five times as long as had been counted on. Some measure of disorganization, loss of impetus and troops, as well as a chance for the opponent to improve his position must be the inevitable result.

In every sense, our military preparations were increased to the utmost. Leave was canceled on all sides; near the frontier, watchfulness was doubled. Roads and bridges could be blown up at a moment's notice; trees were ready to be felled by dynamite with a view to obstructing roads.

How grave the Government thought the situation to be can be no more strikingly illustrated than by the fact that, whereas during the whole war of 1914–18, in which the Netherlands preserved its neutrality, not a strip of land was inundated in order to give support to the army, this time dykes were pierced and large stretches of country were flooded as early as the last days of August. Inundations form a characteristic element in the defenses of Holland. It is a well-known fact that every effort has to be made, day and night, to prevent, through means of powerful pumping installations, large areas of the country from being flooded by the sea or the large rivers, the Rhine, the Meuse and the Yssel. It is extraordinary to see, when comparing a modern map of Holland with one of, let us say, a thousand years ago, how much of the country as it now is, was gradually through arduous toil and great engineering skill reclaimed from the sea, and this reclaiming goes on until the present day. Only a year ago my wife and I motored across country with waving cornfields on either side of the road, over which we had spent many a happy day sailing not five years before when it was still at the bottom of the "Zuyderzee." The picturesque isle of Urk is an isle no longer and is now reached by motor car. Large areas of valuable and fertile land have thus been added to the country—the only way in which Holland ever wishes to increase its "Lebensraum."

This explains why very considerable tracts of land are

below sea level. So large a part does water play in our country that the Netherlands even have a separate Governmental department, with a Cabinet Minister at its head, to deal with "Waterstaat"—the state of the water. Water has had a great influence on the formation of the Dutch national character: it has bred into the Dutch race perseverance, steadfast purpose, patience, endurance and courage. Floods have often in the past ravaged the Dutch countryside; but if to that extent the water has been a constant foe, it was not only by bringing out the qualities just mentioned that this uncertain element has many a time proved itself a benefactor to the people of Holland. For in times of war, inundations have often in history rendered great service to the Dutch. Even for a modern army, as the German campaign in Holland of May, 1940, confirmed, flooded areas are a very serious obstacle; did not the Yser inundations make it possible for the Belgians in the last war to occupy right up to the armistice that last strip of their territory in Flanders where King Albert and his valiant soldiers held their own to the very last?

Inundations, in order to form a military obstacle of the first order, need not be deep; all that is necessary is about four to five feet of water. If barbed wire entanglements are placed on the bottom, that makes them even more effective. This was done by the Dutch wherever the nature of the terrain permitted, and through the engineering skill of the Dutch sappers and the Waterstaat personnel inundations were prepared in places where this was not naturally possible. If, in May, 1940, the German on-slaught on Holland was held up for five days, one of the decisive factors was the fact that the flooded areas made a frontal attack well-nigh impossible.

The mobilization of the Dutch army and navy was completed in four or five successive stages. A surprise attack, a lightning stroke on the part of Germany, or, for that matter, any other power, thus seemed out of the question. It should be emphasized that the Netherlands Government took measures on the sea frontiers as well as on the land frontiers of the country; whereas on the latter the army was conspicuous, our naval forces were prominent along the coast. In this manner the country demonstrated its firm determination to observe a well-balanced neutrality, even before the war around it actually began.

The Bolt from the Blue

THURSDAY the 9th of May passed by without any outward disquieting signs, either at The Hague or in Berlin, until evening fell.

It was a clear spring evening. My wife and I went out for a short walk after dinner, to get some fresh air. It had been a full day, and since my attaché case was not a very heavy one that evening, I hoped to get a good night's rest.

At about nine-thirty—we had just come in—I received a telephone message from the War Office: serious news. There had been a warning, given by our Intelligence Service, of a German attack on the Low Countries; it contained just five words: "Tomorrow at dawn; hold tight."

It was a dreadful moment. Many people may say, "But, after all, you were prepared for that possibility for about nine months, weren't you? And hadn't you had more than one false alarm before?" Of course, all that is perfectly true; but never had the warning come in quite so dramatic and definite a form, nor had we ever had such short notice of impending disaster.

The blow fell on my tiredness with a strangely stimulating effect. It would be an all-night vigil. What scenes would the morrow reveal?

From a military point of view, there was little more that could be done. Every man was at his post, all precautions had been taken. Holland was ready to defend her neutrality to the utmost, her conscience clear.

I conferred by telephone with my colleagues. We arranged that the Defense Minister was to come at once to my house, where we proposed to make our headquarters for the night. Later, events were to prove that we thereby upset plans that had been worked out in every detail and were subsequently found on a captured German general, for German fifth columnists to kidnap Colonel Dijxhoorn, the Minister of Defense, at his home that very night. They had left nothing to chance. Some of the kidnapers were to concentrate on the front entrance to distract the attention of the police on guard in front of the house, while the actual kidnaping was to be done from the garden behind.

In the meantime, the Secretary General of my own department had arrived, together with the Director of the Queen's Cabinet and several other high officials. We sat smoking in my study, feeling strangely calm. The town, too, looked quiet and normal; but we knew that not all its citizens slept, for a precaution never taken before was being carried out that night: thousands of Germans, among whom there might be fifth columnists, were being rounded up. It was a drastic measure which, if this proved to be another false alarm, might cause us considerable embarrassment. But the risk of all these potentially dangerous people being at large could not be taken. Reports came in, meanwhile, from towns all over the country, to the effect that there was not a sign of unrest; absolute quiet reigned everywhere. My wife had the shutters closed, so that late passers-by should not be alarmed by bright lights in the Foreign Minister's official residence at so late an hour.

While The Hague slept, numerous machine-gun posts were being placed on the main roads entering the city, as well as on many bridges and in the neighborhood of important buildings. Similar measures were taken in other cities and villages all over the country. All was done quickly and quietly. General Winkelman, the Commander in Chief, had gone off to inspect his troops. As an additional precaution, a number of minor bridges in Limburg, our southeastern province, were blown up. It was a strange thought to realize that elsewhere, among the civilian population, hardly a soul knew of, and was sharing, our anxieties.

Reports, by telephone and by messenger, kept coming in. The strange thing about them was that when pieced together, they formed anything but a clear picture of what we were to expect. Many, in fact, seemed to indicate that German troops were being drawn away from our frontiers. It was said that they had started holding large-scale manoeuvres from Cleves to Cologne that very afternoon. None of the German barbed-wire entanglements along the Dutch border had been cleared away. No ultimatum or "offer of protection" came, and it was getting late, for a two-hour notice seemed the least they would of their goodness give us. Dawn, so often the herald of Germany's attacks, was less than two hours away. As the long night wore on, some hope came to us once more. To be sure, the situation in Germany behind the frontier was not considered to be quiet, but might not the reported German troop movements be, after all, the prelude to a thrust in the direction of the Balkans? And what was the sense of tiring their men out, as they had done, with marches since the afternoon, if the object was next morning to invade the Netherlands, where they knew they would find considerable resistance? The small hours of the morning found us weary and puzzled, but not without a remnant of hope.

Towards half past two we decided, since there was nothing more that we could usefully do, to try to get some sleep. My Defense colleague was to spend the rest of the night in his office, the others left for their homes, and my wife and I retired to get what sleep we could.

I must have slept fitfully for less than an hour when my wife, too nervous to rest, woke me up. A far-away droning sound was in the air. Was this another accidental violation of our territory? Many a time since then have I marveled at the eagerness with which the human mind is forever inclined to grasp at any last ray of hope.

A minute or so later, before the clock had struck four, the telephone by my bedside rang: there was a report that our airdromes at Waalhaven, Bergen, Schiphol, and de

Kooy had been bombed. While I was trying to get confirmation of this, my wife drew open the curtains and daylight fell, almost surprisingly at this hour of four o'clock, upon us. I had a feeling of numb coldness. Then, suddenly, like a bolt from the blue, hell burst loose around us as the antiaircraft guns came into action against ever-increasing swarms of German planes, bombing barracks on the outskirts of the town. We could see them, as, silhouetted against the blue of our morning sky, they hurled death and destruction upon us—who had never done them or anybody any harm; and who, as their leaders knew only too well, had been neutral in the truest and fullest sense of the word.

Again the telephone rang. Our Minister in Brussels reported that the Belgian capital, too, was being bombed, especially the northern part near the important railway junction of Schaerbeek. He also informed me that German troops had crossed the Luxemburg frontier.

Since there was now a complete certainty of German aggression on Holland, I rang up the Prime Minister and agreed with him that the code word was to be telephoned at once to London and Paris, on receipt of which our Ministers there were to open their secret instructions. By doing this it would be revealed to them that they were to ask Britain and France for help—especially in the air, in view of the disproportion between our own air force and that of the enemy. At the same time they were to give important indications on other points of immediate military interest. Automatically our policy of neutrality had ceased. We had joined the Allies.

Hurriedly my wife and I dressed, while enemy airplanes roared overhead. It had since long been arranged that, in case the worst happened, the Foreign Ministry would be removed to a place less exposed than the center of town where it is normally situated. Since these new quarters were at some considerable distance from the official residence where we lived, we had agreed to borrow a friend's house which was more conveniently situated. Only my wife's faithful maid accompanied us; the other servants received instructions, and off we went by car to our temporary home. It was a very exciting drive, so early in the morning, with antiaircraft guns firing incessantly, some with high-pitched sharp explosions in rapid succession, others booming forth with a heavy sound. Some distance ahead of us a German plane came crashing down in flames; we later heard that it ripped the front off the house of one of the South American diplomats. Military posts were everywhere. Some young soldiers on bicycles came rushing round a street corner, the expression on their red faces at once purposeful and tense, and strangely moving.

We were fortunate in reaching our destination without being hit by falling shrapnel. I left my wife, and went to attend the Cabinet meeting at the Prime Minister's house. It so happened that this was the first Cabinet meeting to be attended by its new member, the Minister for

Agriculture and Fisheries, who had been appointed only a few days before.

Hardly had the meeting begun, when—it must have been towards six o'clock—my secretary telephoned from the Foreign Ministry to say that the German Minister had asked to be given an opportunity of making an important communication; I therefore left at once for my office. Not far from the Royal Palace the car was stopped by soldiers under the command of a young lieutenant, who said that he was unable to let my car through to the center of town. He pointed out that his orders were strict, and very rightly did not give way even when I told him my identity; so I was obliged to leave the car and telephone, in a government office a hundred yards away, for a staff officer to accompany me through the military posts to my office. Just as I was leaving the building, three German planes came swooping down along the street, firing their machine-guns relentlessly while throwing out orange-bordered leaflets, urging the population, incidentally in extremely ungrammatical Dutch, to lay down their arms or else their whole country would have to face thorough destruction. As I took shelter in a doorway I saw them fly over the Palace, aiming at it. Bits of brick and plaster were coming down on all sides, but there were no casualties. This was the first evidence, to my knowledge, of the hunt the Germans lost no time in starting for the Queen, in the same way they had hunted the King of Norway four weeks before.

At about this moment, while swastika planes were dropping death on Holland, the Deutschlandsender in its early morning broadcast was making the following statement:

"The panicky reports about Holland, Belgium, and the Balkans spread by London and Paris are explained by the Paris correspondent of *Il Messagero* as caused by the inner political situation of the Western Powers. Through this creation of rumors, writes the Italian paper, the English and French Governments wish to prevent a cabinet crisis."

As the bombers flew off, I proceeded on my way, this time with a military escort, and soon came to my office. Count von Zech had already arrived, accompanied by two staff officers, enabling him to pass through military cordons.

I saw him at once, and when I set eyes on him I felt truly sorry for the man who had represented Germany at The Hague for more than eleven years. Count von Zech-Burkersroda, to give his full name, a man in his fifties, in whom it was not difficult to detect the cavalry officer he had been in his youth, is the embodiment of a South German landed nobleman. He had married the daughter of the former Chancellor von Bethmann-Holweg, and had been appointed nearly twelve years before by the Government of the Weimar Republic so greatly abhorred by the founders and supporters of the Third Reich. Count von Zech had apparently succeeded in coming to terms with Germany's new masters. What these terms were, we have never known, but we always had the impression that this German diplomat was an honest man, who would not stoop to the use of unfair, or otherwise reprehensible methods. His appearance and behavior on this momentous occasion were in keeping with the opinion we had formed of his character. He seemed deeply moved. As he was, after all, a German, it naturally was very difficult for us to feel whether he felt any justification for the action his Fuehrer was taking. Perhaps he did, perhaps he did not. But I feel sure that Count von Zech was too much of a gentleman not to think of the friendship that had been shown to him by so many people in various walks of life in Holland, who in their turn had received hospitality at the German Legation, and many of whom had become personal friends.

In any case, the German Minister was visibly deeply impressed by the thought that this had to be the termination of his mission to the Netherlands, whose Sovereign, scarcely more than a year before, had bestowed on him the Grand Cross of the Order of Orange-Nassau. The message he now had to deliver was to announce the advance of mighty German armed forces. He was to emphasize that all resistance was completely purposeless. Germany, so the message went on, was ready "to guarantee" the European territories of the Netherlands as well as those in other parts of the world, and also the dynasty, on the condition that no resistance were offered; otherwise—to follow as closely as possible the original German text—the Netherlands would be in danger of seeing the country and its political existence completely annihilated. In view of this, Count von Zech had been ordered to suggest that a pressing appeal should be addressed to the nation and to the military forces, ostensibly—although this was not stated—to abandon all thoughts of resistance; he also was to require that contact be sought with the German Military Command.

Before I could even ask what grounds Germany could possibly have for the callous attack she had launched against a peaceful neutral nation in its sleep, without even any pretense of an ultimatum, previous warning or attempt at negotiation, the German Minister, in a few brief words, gave me those grounds himself. He had instructions to state that the German Government had irrefutable evidence of an immediately threatening invasion by British and French forces in Belgium, the Netherlands and Luxemburg, prepared a long time before with the knowledge of the Netherlands and Belgian Governments. Its aim was, so he said, a thrust at the Ruhr basin.

I looked inquiringly at the German Minister to make sure that he had concluded all he had been told to recite, and then sat thinking for a few moments before making my reply. When he came in I had been intensely curious to hear what he had to say; now I knew. It was a document in the truest Nazi style: the threat was there, the intimidation, the alluring promise, and the false grounds.

It was what had happened to Belgium in 1914 all over again.

It made me very indignant. If there was anyone who knew what pains had incessantly been taken to keep the country in a state of true neutrality, I was that person. No one had toiled and striven more earnestly than I had for more than eight months to take a lead and help in upholding that policy. There, opposite me, sat the representative of Herr Hitler's Government; outside the building, anti-aircraft guns rapped out a sinister accompaniment to our interview. I took a sheet of notepaper and, in order that there should be no misunderstanding, wrote my reply—with the instrument nearest at hand, a blue pencil.

It was very short; it merely said that the Netherlands Government repudiated with indignation the allegation made by Germany that they had in any way, or with any third power, been privy to arrangements directed against Germany. In view of the unprecedented German attack on the Netherlands, it went on, an attack perpetrated without any previous warning, the Netherlands Government considered that a state of war had now arisen between the Kingdom and Germany. I handed this statement to Count von Zech, and asked him whether he had anything further to say. He merely said a few words of farewell. I shook hands with him: I had always thought him a decent man, and even—apart from being a German civil servant—a friend of my country. I shall never be able to forget his slightly bent figure as he left between the staff officers, who escorted him back to the German Legation.

I had a rapid interview with my principal collaborators and with them checked whether all necessary things had been done. Our Legations abroad had been informed; arrangements had been made for the members of the German Legation and German Consulates in the country to be temporarily lodged at the best hotel in The Hague, pending their ultimate destination. This was a difficult problem, for their own army blocked the way to Germany, where they should have gone; Belgium was also involved in the struggle, and the North Sea was quite unsafe for them to traverse. The Director of the Queen's Cabinet arrived; I asked him to inform the Queen, who was then at the Huis ten Bosch, where a bomb-proof shelter had been constructed for her, of the German Minister's message and of my reply.

By that time, I had been summoned to a further Cabinet meeting in one of the other Government buildings, perhaps a mile from the Foreign Office. The streets presented an extraordinary sight. It was about 7 o'clock, a beautiful sunny day. The flowering shrubs in the park through which I had to pass were blooming profusely. All the people I saw in the streets were admirable in their steadiness and utter lack of panic. By bicycle or on foot, they calmly went off to their work, looking up now and then at the German planes circling overhead. At all important crossings, groups of soldiers with machine guns

and rifles stopped all cars and passers-by, to find out
whether there were any Germans among them and search
them if necessary. Now and again a loud explosion rent
the air. The enemy was apparently dropping bombs in
the neighborhood, although it was difficult to see for
what reason, since The Hague was an open town with a
garrison of but very slight importance. Perhaps one might
have forgiven them if they had only bombed the barracks, the only target of a military nature in the town
except the buildings of the Defense Ministry and the
General Staff; but their aiming was extremely inaccurate,
perhaps owing to the constant fire of our antiaircraft batteries which forced them to stay at a considerable altitude. Instead of a military objective, one bomb destroyed
part of a maternity hospital, killing and wounding nurses,
young mothers, and babies and at the same time destroying the façade of a row of houses adjoining a prison
nearby.

Let us now for a few minutes leave the Cabinet to its
discussions and see what in the meantime was happening
in Berlin. There, at 5.30 A. M. a subordinate diplomatic official had asked to see Jonkheer van Haersma de With,
who, before his appointment to the Legation in Berlin,
had been the Queen's Envoy to Washington. The Minister was requested to call on Herr von Ribbentrop at
once.

The meeting took place at 6.15 A. M. when the German
Minister for Foreign Affairs handed the Netherlands Min-

ister a voluminous memorandum with annexes which he was asked to read. Jonkheer van Haersma de With began reading these documents, and his indignation increased with his astonishment as he turned the fifty-nine pages of this paper. When he was ready, he indignantly refuted the allegations it contained, an easy task in view of the patently false character of the arguments.

Perhaps the reader will ask: "But what were these documents?" They started with the assertion that the principal purpose of French and British policy was the extension of the war to more and more countries, which were to be used as auxiliaries of the Western Powers. Germany had only just prevented this policy from succeeding in Norway, and had now found herself obliged to take precautionary action in the Netherlands and Belgium (Luxemburg apparently was so small that it had been overlooked in this document). For Belgium and Holland had not been neutral, so these papers alleged. Since the war began, Belgian and Dutch newspapers had been even more hostile to Germany than the French and British papers; prominent people in both countries had shown that sympathies in the Low Countries were with England and France; many other happenings, of a political and economic nature, were said to have accentuated this tendency. It was remarkable that not a single concrete instance of these accusations was mentioned, nor was the question raised as to how far these statements had any bearing on neutrality as defined by international law. One thing is certain: if this line of argument had any value at all, it is difficult to see why the Germans did not at once declare war on the United States.

Furthermore, the documents said, the Netherlands had supported the British Secret Service in attempts to stir up revolution in Germany, with the active collaboration of the very highest civil servants and army staffs. Then, the precautions taken by the Governments of Belgium and the Netherlands were said to be irrefutable evidence of the fact that both countries had taken military measures against Germany only, in order to assert their neutrality by force of arms. In the case of the Netherlands in particular, this was a flagrant lie: facing England were troops all along the coast in sufficient numbers to prevent any landings, and in addition there was the navy.

In this strain the German memorandum went on, corroborated by long and extremely confused reports by Himmler, the notorious and dreaded chief of the Gestapo, the Nazi Minister for the Interior, Dr. Frick, and the Head of the Army High Command, General Keitel. The sphere in which these documents had been drawn up can perhaps best be characterized by a verbatim quotation from the final paragraph of the report signed by Himmler and Frick, which said that they hoped to obtain more light on the "dark plans of the obscure, homosexual, yea even a-social criminal elements of the so-called Secret Intelligence Service." It was a style reminiscent of the columns of Soviet newspapers.

The document [1] had obviously been pasted together from various elements. It was confused and redundant in its statement of facts. This may have been done on purpose, for it was obviously not intended to be simple and plain, but to form a barrage of massed detail which was to achieve a cumulative effect.

It is a curious thing that at The Hague no copy of these documents was available to be handed to those whom they chiefly concerned: the Netherlands Government. The German Minister did not possess such a copy. This was no

---

[1] On June 28, 1940, the Germans published a "White Book" containing documents alleged "to have been picked out at random from the masses of evidence seized by German troops during their advance through Holland and Belgium," to show that the Government of the Netherlands "had made detailed military arrangements with Britain and France." For anyone interested in the technique of German propaganda, it may be worth-while to examine this "White Book." For all others such examination must be loss of time, since the Netherlands had made no previous military arrangements of any kind with France and Britain.

What the Germans chiefly relied upon were the contents of the sealed instructions of a military nature that had been sent in good time to the Dutch Legations in Paris and London to be opened only on receipt of a code word, which was to be sent only in the case of a German attack. By omitting the essential statement that these instructions were not previously known to anyone outside the Dutch High Command, not even to the Ministers of the Netherlands in Paris and London who had them (sealed) in their safe keeping, the false impression was created that arrangements of a military character had been made between the Netherlands and the Allies. When the German White Book was published, the Dutch Commander in Chief, General Winkelman, drew attention to this insidious omission calculated to create the impression that the Netherlands Government had been guilty of a grave breach of neutrality. As a result the General was relieved of his post as Commander in Chief and taken to Germany as a prisoner of war. But his chief purpose had been successful: the German White Book was discredited.

accident, as those less familiar with methods used by the Third Reich might think. Herr von Ribbentrop, when he saw the Netherlands Minister in the early hours of Friday morning, stated expressly that his memorandum with its annexes was not to be presented at The Hague. Surely, to the ordinary mind, this was a most extraordinary procedure. The whole fabrication purported to be an indictment of the Netherlands Government, the Dutch civil and military authorities and the nation as a whole. But they were to be attacked first; they were not even to be told immediately after the attack was launched, what grievances the Germans had against them, and all they were allowed to learn was from Dr. Goebbels' broadcast of these accusations, while the onslaught was in progress. The radio is, after all, an instrument admitting of no discussion, like the Nazi Government itself, which, in international relations, has a particular liking for action without previous negotiation. Herr von Ribbentrop's typescript had obviously been prepared well in advance, ready to be used when occasion should require: the annex signed by Himmler and Frick was dated as far back as March 29th. It seems singular that the Germans did not think twice before using a six-weeks-old document in order to prove—"irrefutably"—the necessity of forestalling a Franco-British attempt at invading Germany which, according to Herr von Ribbentrop in his memorandum bearing the date of May 9th, was only then imminent, and of which nobody had had any previous indication. The whole aim of this amazing collection of falsehoods and distortions was plain. Acting on Hitler's tenet that small lies are unconvincing, whereas big lies, especially if repeated often enough, always find a hearing, the Nazis had prepared a "dossier" against the Netherlands. This dossier, composed with true German thoroughness, was to be ready in good time so that it might be pulled out of a drawer at a moment when the leaders gave the signal. One of the chief arguments relied on for use against Holland was the Venlo incident. It goes without saying that this incident, which took place, it will be remembered, in November, 1939, would have been used at once if the Germans had at that time been in need of any so-called excuse for attacking Holland: nothing essential had since changed in the relations between the two countries. But no; the tale, as distorted and exaggerated by the Germans, was carefully put into cold storage; warmed up in March by Frick and Himmler; found insufficient by the central leaders when they thought the time to use it was approaching; developed, therefore, by General Keitel's collaborators in the form of a memorandum dated May 5th, and finally summarized, condensed, and provided with headlines by Herr von Ribbentrop in the document he presented to the Dutch envoy.

We have here a typical example of Nazi tactics: summary action without previous discussion. Relying on superior force, the Nazi acts as judge and jury, meting out punishment in controversies in which he is one of the par-

ties concerned. Truly it is difficult to find a more complete
reversal of the normal standards of civilized communities.
Woe betide the world in which the Nazi, with this retro-
grade conception of international intercourse, holds a
dominating position. Here is a demonstration *ad oculos*
of what the democracies stand for—and are fighting for.

The loose reasoning, the references to witnesses who—
so these documents naïvely stated—had either died or were
languishing in Gestapo prisons, the absence of names and
further particulars of informants merely described as "a
reliable source" or other similar indications—all this contributed towards giving this singular impeachment a very
doubtful character, even to the uninitiated. The initiated
know that there is no foundation for any such accusations.
Never had the Dutch Government had any knowledge of
a French, or a British, or a Franco-British plan to invade
Germany; never have staff talks been held between the
Netherlands and any Allied country or countries. The
Netherlands Government as well as the whole nation had
a clear conscience. It was that clear conscience which
made them resist the German aggression with all the force
they could command, knowing that they were the victims of an outrage.

Herr von Ribbentrop's diatribes became very unconvincing when, in their final passages, in spite of all Belgian
and Dutch misdeeds, they fell back on the anticlimax that
the German army merely came to safeguard the neutrality
of these criminal countries with all the military forces of

the Reich; Herr von Ribbentrop then went on: "The German forces have not come as enemies of the Belgian and Dutch nation, for the Government of the Reich has not wanted or caused this development." One rubs one's eyes when reading such statements, and it seems best to waste no more words on the German indictment, but to dismiss it with La Rochefoucauld's saying that: "Hypocrisy is homage paid by vice to virtue."

After the Netherlands Minister had categorically and vehemently repudiated the allegations contained in Herr von Ribbentrop's documents, the latter made a pressing appeal to abandon all resistance in Holland. He said that the Fuehrer was a good friend, but a dangerous foe; he was ready to guarantee the independence of the Netherlands, including the overseas territories, and the dynasty, on the sole condition that the Dutch were to give up defending themselves. Unless they gave it up at once, "Vernichtung"—annihilation—would be their fate. The Netherlands envoy coolly replied that he had nothing to add to his previous declarations, to the effect that his country would resist to the utmost, and that history would hold Germany alone responsible for this unprovoked attack on a friendly nation. Herewith the interview came to an end; Jonkheer van Haersma de With was escorted back to the Legation, where he learned that Holland considered herself at war with Germany.

Cut off from all communication with The Hague, the

Minister decided to ask for his passports in order to leave
Germany by way of Switzerland, at the same time taking
the opportunity of renewing his protests against Germany's action. At three o'clock in the afternoon, his note
was handed in at the German Foreign Ministry. A few
hours later, the Counsellor of the Legation was summoned
to come at once to the Foreign Office. After having been
kept waiting for a long time—so long that he finally signified his intention of leaving if he were held up any
longer—he was told that the note in which the Minister
had asked for his passports could not be accepted because
of what was described as its "insolent character." When
the Dutch diplomat asked why the German Government
took offense at the note, the official who received him said
that Herr von Ribbentrop had been displeased by a paragraph saying: "Violating the elementary principles of
right and decency, Germany has torn asunder the ancient
links by which it was bound to the Dutch nation in peace
and friendship," and especially by the expression "Germany's aggression." When the Dutchman remarked that
in this case the word "aggression" seemed hardly out of
place, the German official curtly replied: "This is no case
of aggression," and when asked how Germany's action
was then to be described, merely shrugged his shoulders
saying: "That is not what we are discussing at present."
Their rejection of the Dutch Minister's note did not prevent the German Foreign Office from carefully keeping a

copy of it, and next morning, large headlines in the Berlin papers announced to the public the "shocking insolence of the Dutch war criminals," and "crooks" who had dared to call Germany's action by its true name.

Pending their departure for Switzerland, the Dutch Minister and his staff remained in Berlin, where, for the first day or so, they were left at liberty. Then, however, they were all consigned to the Legation building, which was quite unfit for housing an additional thirty people, some of them with small children. The American Chargé d'Affaires, Mr. Alexander Kirk, and the Swedish Minister fortunately saw to it that sufficient mattresses were obtained and that meals were provided, for nobody was allowed to leave the building, which was surrounded by Gestapo and completely isolated, as the telephone had been cut off. No excuse or explanation was given for this unusually harsh treatment. Finally, in the evening of the fourth day, a special train took the party to the Lake of Constance on the Swiss frontier, from which place, after another five days of waiting—in a comfortable hotel this time—they were at last allowed to leave the country. On the far side of Lake Constance, a warm welcome awaited them on Swiss territory, and no kindness was ever more appreciated than the care they received in the small Confederation, where liberty, truth, and honor rank as highly as they do in Holland.

In Berlin, the news of the German offensive against

Holland and Belgium was received without any enthusi-
asm by the man in the street. The general mood remained
as depressed as before. For some strange reason, dancing
was suddenly prohibited.

Meanwhile enemy aircraft were hurling death and destruction on the Netherlands. While the Cabinet was ex-
amining reports on the fighting which were constantly
coming in, the Queen made a stirring appeal in a broadcast to the whole world. "After our country, with scrupulous conscientiousness, has observed strict neutrality during all these months," Her Majesty said, "Germany has
made a sudden attack on our territory without any warning. This was done notwithstanding a solemn promise
that the neutrality of our country would be respected so
long as we maintained that neutrality. I herewith direct a
flaming protest against this unprecedented violation of
good faith and of all that is decent in relations between
cultured States. I and my Government now will do our
duty." The message stirred the hearts of everyone, at
home as well as abroad.

The Government soon began to receive reports of a
particularly alarming nature. Telephone messages coming
in from many places around The Hague revealed that
parachutists had landed in a wide circle surrounding the
seat of the Government. These men were dropped from
especially designed airplanes: the pilot, when finding himself above the indicated spot, merely had to pull a lever

by his side in order to cause the bottom of the plane to open up, thereby dropping the parachutists out into space. These men carried not only small firearms but also machine guns and radio sets. Upon landing, they took cover behind dykes, in woods, or in farmhouses, and by their considerable number soon became a constant and highly dangerous nuisance, terrorizing the countryside and causing a great dispersal of troops required to deal with them. These parachutists, youths between 16 and 20 years of age, stop at nothing, steeped as they are in the doctrine that anything is permissible in a war waged for the glory of Germany. In addition, we learned that large numbers of troops were being landed from hydroplanes coming down on canals, docks, and rivers in the heart of the country, particularly in the immediate vicinity of Rotterdam and its airdrome of Waalhaven.

After violent aerial combats from which the German forces, vastly outnumbering the Dutch, emerged victorious, they were able to machine-gun the Dutch battalions defending the airdromes, thereby causing very heavy losses. Parachutists were then dropped to remove the obstacles placed on the landing fields, and from that moment on the enemy was also able to bring up troops in land planes. Within a few hours after the attack began, this had taken place at Waalhaven near Rotterdam, as well as at three smaller airdromes near The Hague, and in that way thousands of German soldiers were soon forming up in a circle around the country's political and administrative nerve center. The purpose was clear. As in Norway, the invader's first aim was to paralyze at once the activities of the Queen and Government. This needed little confirmation. It was obvious to anyone casting a look on the map of Holland.

The valor of the Dutch troops, who in their fury fought as only men defending their own country in a good cause can fight, in one day suppressed the danger of Queen and Government being taken prisoner almost before the battle had developed.

Later in the same day, an aircraft was shot down transporting a German General, who was killed. His instructions were found on him. These proved that General von Sponeck—for that was his name—had orders to take The Hague on the first day of the invasion. If the Dutch gave in, he was to treat them as the Danes had been treated a month before. In that case, careful provisions were to be made for placing a guard of honor before the Royal Palace. If, however, the Dutch persisted in defending their country, the Queen and her Ministers were to be sent, as soon as possible, to Berlin by transport plane, where, it was stated, they were to be dealt with in accordance with their refusal to surrender.

These plans were frustrated. At the hour when, according to the German time table, The Hague was to have fallen into their hands, General von Sponeck lay dead. The parade uniform which he had taken good care to bring with him, would serve him no more. Even the horse on which he had planned to make a triumphant entry into The Hague had shared his master's fate.

Escape to London

THE Dutch Cabinet now took a momentous decision. The voice of the lawful Netherlands Government must in no case be silenced, even if the worst should happen. Nothing might be left undone to ensure this. There was, of course, no question of the Government as a whole leaving the country at this juncture, although they were in danger of being captured. The actual battle had only just begun, and the possibility was by no means excluded that our forces might prove able to hold their own. But some precaution seemed imperative in the circumstances and it was therefore decided that the Ministers for Foreign Affairs and for the Colonies were to make an attempt to leave the country at once for Allied territory, and establish contact with the Governments of Britain and France. Mr. Welter and I therefore rose and took leave of our colleagues. We needed little time to make our plan. As fighting was then going on between The Hague and Rotterdam and even beyond, it seemed unlikely that a journey to France by way of Western Belgium would be possible. All airdromes in the neighborhood being no longer available, a seaplane seemed our only chance. Luck was with us. On ninety-nine days out of a hundred, the sea breaks on the coast of Holland in heavy rollers, making it impossible for a hydroplane to lie at anchor any-where near the shore; but this was the hundredth day. Scarcely a ripple marred the water's surface. The Naval Staff was therefore asked to send a seaplane to Scheve-ningen, the seaside resort immediately adjoining The Hague, while we rapidly prepared ourselves for the jour-ney. I found my wife and asked her whether, in case the hydroplane had room for her as well as for my colleague and myself, she was willing to take the risk of coming with me. She at once assented. We hurriedly packed a few pa-pers and personal belongings, and with my colleague drove to Scheveningen. It was a strange scene. The Naval Staff had sent two hydroplanes, which lay riding at anchor on the blue water. Firing was going on all about us, from the harbor piers, from near the lighthouse and from the prom-enade, in an attempt to keep the German aircraft, several of which were hovering above the town, from swooping down on ours. We were escorted across the sandy beach by some high officers, who told us that both hydroplanes had already been shot at on their way to Scheveningen by parachutists with heavy machine guns. One of them was losing fuel at such a rate that it was unfit for use, but the other one, although it had a leak in one of its floats, seemed able to take off. The commander said there would be room for my wife, so we clambered on board, where we sat wedged in beside the machine gun, the wireless set and other warplane equipment. Half of our modest lug-gage found a place on board; the rest had to be left behind.

The cannonade around us continued. The engines were started up, but only after several vain attempts which made the minutes seem like hours. Finally we took off, bumped hard several times on the water as the heavily laden plane gathered speed, and then rose from the water. The engines' roar drowned all other sounds as we steered our course seaward, later following the coastline, flying low above the sea during the whole voyage. Soon nothing was in sight except a few scattered fishing smacks whose crews waved at us, wondering no doubt whether to try and return to port or stay at sea while the battle on land and in the air was in progress. As we flew on across the wide expanse of water, gleaming in the sunlight which it reflected, it seemed as if some padded door had been closed between us and the land we had just left. The staccato sound of the antiaircraft guns was gone; in comparison, the continuous droning of our engines was a soothing sound.

We never realized at the time how narrow our escape had been. One of the officers who had escorted us to the water's edge told us three days later in London that within two minutes after we had taken off, a German dive bomber swooped down, in spite of the antiaircraft barrage, towards the damaged seaplane we had left behind, lying at anchor twenty yards from where we had lain. It was hit and sunk; the three occupants, keen young sailors, to whom we had been talking a few minutes before, were killed.

The journey seemed uneventful. Our pilot had instructions to take us to an air base on the south coast of England. The difficulty proved to be how to find that place: our trip had been hurriedly improvised, so much so that there was no map on board covering the whole journey. We decided to do the best we could, and headed for the Straits of Dover, which we passed at about equal distance between France and England. I was thinking of what we would have to do once we arrived in London, and scribbled on the back of an envelope some notes for a broadcast I hoped to be given an opportunity of making that evening. We were flying above the Channel when the pilot discovered that our fuel level was sinking rapidly, more rapidly in fact than was normal. Had the gas tank been hit as well as the float? We realized there was not much time for reflection. On our starboard was a large town, and we decided to come down on the sea—just as smooth there as it had been near our own coast. On landing, we taxied towards the shore. Apparently the British coastguard understood that we were in distress, for no aircraft took off to intercept us; in order to signify our peaceful intentions, the wireless operator had climbed onto our wing, waving my white handkerchief. As we approached land a large crowd was collecting on the beach, and it was not long before we were able to distinguish several policemen among them. When at last our seaplane, heeling over a good deal more than when we

took off two hours before, ran aground on the pebbly
shore, they assisted us in getting on land while two or
three kind people took charge of our unimpressive lug-
gage. We were told that we had landed at Brighton. At
the Brighton Chief Constable's office, our scanty papers
were inspected and, although they were quite insufficient
according to normal standards, they were accepted after
a telephone conversation with our Legation in London.
It was by then 1 o'clock in the afternoon, and we had had
nothing to eat since the previous evening; the tea and
sandwiches which the kind Chief Constable had sent for
were nectar and ambrosia to us. A train was about to leave
for London; it was held up for a few moments to enable
us to catch it. The Brighton police provided us with
tickets—for we had no English money—and accompanied
by the Mayor of Brighton we left for our destination. All
were most kind. Somehow it seemed a dream. The peaceful English countryside was so very different from the
scenes of violence and destruction we had just left.

Two members of the Dutch Government were now in
London, where they could take up contact at once with
the British Government and, through the French Em-
bassy, with the Government of France. Whatever happened, the Germans could no longer succeed in their desperate attempt to silence the lawful Government of
Holland. This thought gave my colleague and myself a
feeling of deep satisfaction, and the warm welcome our

Minister and his Staff gave us soon made us forget some
of the strain we had gone through in the last twenty-four
hours.

Lord Halifax, on whom we called the same afternoon,
welcomed us at the Foreign Office with equal cordiality
and we discussed with him and some of his officials various
matters which had to be taken in hand at once. In this respect also, the decision the Government had taken of
sending my colleague and myself over proved to be invaluable. Through the kindness of the British Broadcasting Corporation, I had a chance of saying that evening to
the British people that we had come to establish a firm
contact, in the name of the Netherlands Government,
with the Governments of those powers whose Allies we
had become. That contact was intensified, in the course
of the next few days, by numerous discussions with members of the British Government, and with the Naval, Military, and Air Force Staffs. With our heart in Holland,
and our head in London, we had the feeling of being useful to those whom we had left behind. Special mention
should be made of the gracious kindness shown to us by
His Majesty the King. Mr. Welter and I were both received in audience the day after our arrival, and were
deeply touched by the sincere interest the King took in
the fate that had befallen our country and the admiration
he expressed for the gallantry of our fighting forces.

As soon as the most pressing affairs had been seen to,
my colleague and I flew to Paris, little thinking as we

crossed the French coastline south of Dieppe that within a month from that day the Germans would already have occupied that little seaside resort.

Paris seemed almost deserted. We were received in audience by the President of the Republic, whose great personal charm and simplicity are very striking. Useful contacts were established with several of the Cabinet Ministers, among them M. Paul Reynaud, at that time head of the Government and Minister for Foreign Affairs. We also received the French and the foreign press, and were given the opportunity of broadcasting to the French nation. During the few days we spent in France, we tried to do all that might be helpful for establishing a close and cordial contact with our French Ally.

As we had decided to take up temporary residence in London, the time soon came to return to England. Our journey was more difficult this time, for the air route was said to be unsafe; we decided to go by boat from Le Havre. The wife of the Counsellor of our Legation in Paris offered to drive us there, and we arrived just in time to board the steamer, which was packed with people returning to England. Many of them had come from Italy, which then was on the verge of taking part in the conflict after an unedifying calculation as to which side she considered most likely to win. The throb of the ship's engines, as we left the quayside, was accompanied by the sinister wailing of sirens heralding an air attack.

In Holland, the bitter struggle had come to an end.

Germany had drawn a curtain of steel between that unhappy country and the outside world. For the time being, Holland was in Hitler's grip.

The Juggernaut Rolls

THE German campaign in the Netherlands reveals more than one novel method of warfare. It also affords striking illustration of the tactics used by the Germans for undermining the power of resistance of their victims by fifth-column activity prior to the actual outbreak of hostilities, activity which is followed by open support to the invader as soon as war has actually begun.

In evidence of their scrupulous policy of neutrality the Netherlands had disposed its forces in such a manner that both sea and land frontiers were given adequate protection on all sides. It is obvious that in order to obtain a true image of these well-balanced military measures against attack, from whatever side it might come, it is necessary to take into account not only the land forces, but also the navy, as these two elements, together with the air force, form a whole. The coastal line was guarded in the first place by the navy with its surface vessels, submarines, seaplanes and minefields; in addition, there was a whole army corps distributed along the seaboard of Holland proper—the two northwestern provinces which form the heart of the country—and further army units on all the islands of the province of Zeeland. The southern provinces, bordering on Belgium, held a considerable number of troops, and on the remaining front, facing Germany, were two army corps in the central section, with more troops to the south of these. By this distribution of the Kingdom's armed forces, equilibrium was obtained with regard to both belligerent parties. In February, 1940, a party of about forty American, Japanese, Belgian, Italian, Swiss, Hungarian, Yugoslav, and Rumanian journalists had been authorized in the course of a three-day excursion to see these dispositions on the spot.

The Germans, notably General Keitel in his report mentioned heretofore, have attempted to show that Dutch military measures were not balanced with regard to both belligerent parties; for this purpose they completely ignored the considerable part played by the navy in our coastal defenses. In view of this, it seems hardly necessary to give more attention to this unfair way of describing the position. Impartial observers are agreed that the disposition of Holland's armed forces was a true reflection of the policy of neutrality which the Dutch have, from the beginning to the very last, so consistently upheld.

As an introductory phase to their attack, the Germans began, during the early hours of Friday, May 10th, to lay magnetic mines in the mouths of our large rivers and harbor entrances, followed shortly afterwards by bomb and machine-gun attacks on a number of military airdromes. Guided by lessons learnt in Norway, the Dutch had taken the precaution of leaving no airplanes in the hangars, but had placed them alongside the landing fields, on nearby roads, and on auxiliary airdromes prepared with the greatest possible secrecy. Thanks to these measures, the result of the early bombing attacks on hangars was negligible; on the other hand, the German machine-gun attacks on the Dutch airplanes left out in the open, before they were all able to take off, disabled a great number of them.

Unfortunately, the Dutch had not yet been able to complete the measures planned after the invasion of Norway for the protection of their flying fields; had these been ready, they would have made it exceedingly difficult for the enemy to gain a foothold there. As it was, the detachments guarding the airdromes were an easy prey for the low-flying German aircraft sent to destroy them. With the aid of parachutists who cleared away the obstacles on these fields as soon as they had been landed, three airdromes around The Hague—Iepenburg, Valkenburg and Ockenburg—fell early the first morning into the hands of the enemy, who at once started landing numerous troop-carrying airplanes on the spaces cleared.

As early as 5 A. M. the enemy had by this method completely encircled the seat of the Government. Thus, while in the east the Germans advanced towards the positions designed to stem their attack, they simultaneously and with great vigor attacked the heart of the country and its very nerve center from the air, seriously threatening the communications between the seat of the Dutch Government and High Command and the rest of the country. An attempt followed at intimidating the population of

The Hague, which, although it completely failed to achieve its purpose, resulted in considerable damage. At 5 o'clock that morning, incendiary bombs were dropped on the northern part of the town; at the same time, high-explosive bombs were aimed—fortunately, very badly—at the buildings of the Naval Staff. Other German aircraft flew low above the town, rattling their machine guns at random with a complete disregard for the civilian population, which is strikingly illustrated by the fact that in the attractive residential quarter of Marlot, lying isolated at some distance from The Hague, where there are no military objectives whatsoever, several people were killed and houses damaged by bullets.

At 10 A. M. a second bombing attack followed, this time on the center of town. Scores of enemy planes, meanwhile, were falling prey to our antiaircraft artillery, and the fact deserves special mention that the largest daily "bag" of enemy aircraft since the beginning of war in September, was obtained that day by the Dutch—well over one hundred were brought down, a truly magnificent record. But even this result, favorable as it was, did not fail to cause havoc. To quote one instance only, a large three-engined aircraft was brought down in flames near the outskirts of town; one of its engines fell, with a deafening crash, in the middle of a street, while its burning wreckage set several houses on fire, the inhabitants' shrieks being drowned by the roar of the flames. The pilot's body was found—he was a youth of seventeen.

Before proceeding with a description of the activities of our land forces, a tribute of deep admiration should be paid to the Dutch Air Force, whose young and courageous pilots, although vastly outnumbered, played their gallant part until the very last. Every one of our airplanes was lost. The man who took the last remaining Dutch aircraft up, announced to his comrades his intention of dropping his load of bombs on Waalhaven airdrome—then occupied by the Germans—knowing full well that he would never return.

The primary task of the Netherlands Commander in Chief, General Winkelman, was to ascertain the purpose of the enemy. Was his object to invade the whole country, or was his chief aim to force a passage through the southern provinces on his way to Belgium and France? It soon became apparent that Herr Hitler's troops had been ordered to occupy the whole country, from the point where, in the north, the frontier reaches the sea, to its southernmost extremity. As a result, the Dutch forces were faced with a threefold task, namely to resist:

1) an advance in the north, which, if the enemy succeeded in moving up along the broad dyke closing in the Zuyderzee and connecting the provinces of Friesland and Northern Holland, would constitute a threat against the center of the country;

2) a more direct attack on the center of the country, for which the enemy would have to attempt to traverse the inundated belt in the east and south; and

3) an advance through the provinces of Limburg and Brabant, followed by fanwise operations in the direction of the heart of the country, the extreme southwest, and Belgium.

Those sections of the army facing the German frontier would naturally have to bear the whole brunt of the first onslaught by the German land forces. It had been anticipated that, in case of a German attack, the First Army Corps, and further units, whose task it had been during the period of neutrality to guard part of the coast, would be able to act as a reserve for strengthening any weak spots which might become apparent in the east.

This fundamental plan was entirely frustrated by the landing of thousands of German air-borne troops in the center of the country near The Hague and Rotterdam, supported by the activity of parachutists and of the fifth column, of which we shall hear more later on.

Early in the morning of the fatal day it had already become clear that, in addition to an attempt to paralyze the action of the Government and High Command, the German Staff wished to possess themselves at the earliest possible moment of the important bridges in Rotterdam and at the Moerdijk, which form the connection between Holland proper and the approach to Belgium and France through the southern province of Brabant. The German troops, landing in great numbers in hydroplanes on the broad river running through Rotterdam and on the waters near the Moerdijk, succeeded in taking by surprise the two main bridges across the Meuse as well as the great Moerdijk bridge, all of which are of vital importance. The reader will wish to know why these bridges were not blown up in time. The reply is that although some bridges were blown up, others were taken by treachery, by means of German troops in disguise. It will be recalled that, several months before, the authorities had discovered cases of smuggling into Germany of all kinds of Dutch uniforms. It now became clear what these uniforms were wanted for. The German soldiers carrying out these operations wore uniforms which even to the trained eye were indistinguishable, before it was too late, from Dutch uniforms. Many parachutists came disguised as policemen or postmen, civilians, tram conductors, or even as women. Among them were former German maidservants who, landing in the neighborhood of homes that had once employed them, made themselves useful as guides for other parachutists. These methods, employed by the Germans contrary to all usages of warfare, had some fatal results. Among others, it became known that a group of about a hundred Germans disguised as Dutch soldiers managed unobserved to join ranks behind a Dutch battalion advancing in the dunes. All of a sudden they opened fire on the Dutch, causing heavy losses before they could be overpowered. Other disguised Germans sought cover behind women or groups of children, whom they drove before them.

Parties of these disguised German soldiers would ap-

proach groups of genuine Dutch soldiers, who, unaware
of having to do with the enemy, were attacked by surprise under cover of these abominable tactics. One of
the strategically most important bridges, the Moerdijk
bridge, was taken by the Germans in this way before it
could be blown up. A party of disguised Germans drove
onto it in lorries commandeered after alighting from an
airplane, approached the detachment guarding the bridge
who thought they were coming as reinforcements, shot
them down to the last man and, before the explosive
charges hidden in the pillars of the bridge could be fired,
were masters of the situation. It was a German success,
but a success obtained through means condemned by the
laws of war observed by all civilized nations, and which
no country will envy the Third Reich.

Then there were the parachutists. Besides the part they
took, as we have seen, in capturing airdromes, their task
was to cause confusion, to terrorize the countryside, to
make it necessary for the Dutch army to scatter its reserves in order to deal with them, and to endanger communications. Perhaps the following account by an eye-
witness will, better than any military handbook, give the
reader an idea of how this element of considerable nuisance value operates.

Our witness had spent the night between Thursday and
Friday in some town in the south of the country. He was
awakened, so he said, towards dawn, by the droning of
airplanes accompanied by the rattle of machine guns and

antiaircraft artillery. The thought of manoeuvres flashed through his mind.

Our witness, a man with a university education, rang up the porter of his hotel. "War!" was the reply, "Germany is attacking us!"

He dressed rapidly. The dining room was full of people talking excitedly. There were two young men he knew, who wished to make an attempt at reaching Rotterdam; would he come with them? The offer was gratefully accepted, and soon the party was on its way.

There was a radio in the car and as they drove along they heard the Queen's stirring appeal to the world. Before long, the huge girders of the Moerdijk bridge, spanning one of Holland's broadest rivers, loomed in the distance. They saw three cars halting on the road ahead of them, their occupants waving at them to make them stop.

"Are you in such a hurry to get rid of your car?"

"What do you mean?"

"If you go along for another two hundred yards you will find the Germans!"

This sounded ridiculous. Germans in this westerly part of the country? What about our own defenses? Had they been broken through within a few hours? At that moment one of the party drew their attention to an enemy airplane flying high overhead, beneath which a number of small white clouds were seen slowly descending in the sunlight.

"Parachutists, look!"

But they seemed far away. Our party decided to run the risk and drove on. After another few hundred yards, however, on rounding a bend, they came across a row of empty cars, and a figure in the middle of the road held up his hand.

"Halt! Aussteigen! Put your car there!" The soldier, a tall disheveled-looking boy, wearing a small helmet of a peculiar shape, was dressed in the garb of a German parachutist; he held a pistol in his hand and carried a number of hand grenades in his belt.

Apparently the parachutists were out for motor cars, not for their occupants. Our witness and his friends walked away without being molested. Further on they saw a large group of these soldiers, in their midst a couple of Dutch soldiers they had taken prisoner. A little further on lay the uniformed body of a young Dutchman, his pale face turned towards the sky, a large pool of blood around him—a symbol of his country, attacked by ruthless superior force.

These parachutists, reckless young fellows between the ages of 16 and 20, gave a lot of work to the First Army Corps, and prevented it from being useful elsewhere. Each small group—they were let down in groups of twenty or thirty—carried automatic weapons which in some cases they fired even before landing; each group had to be mopped up separately. Cases are on record in which farmhouses, used by these men as small fortresses, had to be shelled by field guns in order to get rid of them, thereby burying under the ruins not only the invaders but also the unfortunate inhabitants, killed by the gunfire of their own countrymen. In the end, the Dutch succeeded in getting rid of them. By that time, however, operations in other parts of the country had developed to such an extent that this mopping up could not alter the final outcome of the struggle.

Worse even than the parachutists' action, and far more reprehensible, were the activities of the so-called fifth column; a term which, unknown little more than three years ago, in these days has the doubtful honor of being understood by everybody.

In order to comprehend the full importance of this insidious element in Holland, it should be mentioned that for a great many years past there always have been thousands of German residents in that country. As we have seen, many of them had after one or two generations become completely assimilated with the population; others, however, and more especially those who were first settlers, continued to feel themselves real Germans and had not given up allegiance to the Vaterland. Before the Nazi regime came into power in 1933, this state of affairs gave no rise to alarm, but when Herr Hitler began organizing the "Auslandsdeutschtum" there was in many countries reason for serious misgivings. In Holland the authorities had abundant evidence that the leaders of the German colony—people in all walks of life but each with an appointed place in the vast Nazi organization—brought considerable pressure to bear on their compatriots, forcing them to take part in activities directed against the security of the country whose hospitality many of them had enjoyed for years. Only a few days before the German attack, the President of the German Chamber of Commerce for the Netherlands, himself a German who had resided in Holland for twenty years, was found by the police to be in possession of a complete, but inaccurate, plan of the Dutch inundations, which he had been forced by one of the German espionage organizations to obtain. In a provincial town a German chemist had been summoned to some German society in Rotterdam, where he was told that he was to engage in espionage work; it was made quite clear to him what the consequences would be if he refused. There were any number of such cases. The object of this shady work was by no means solely the collecting of military information. These same people were provided with arms, to be used in accordance with detailed instructions when the hour struck. The odious character of this action becomes apparent to the full when it is remembered that the official German "Auslandsorganisation" is always proclaiming that it is the first commandment for any German living abroad to respect the laws of the country affording him hospitality. What is thus proclaimed aloud is disclaimed in secret. Any decent German showing hesitation in lending himself to such practices is soon reminded of the fact that the terrorism which has enslaved the German at home can very easily reach him outside his country, either directly or vicariously in the person of his relations in the Reich.

But there is yet another fifth column, at least as dangerous. It consists of those citizens of a country whose minds have been seduced by the ideology of totalitarianism. If they find that the majority of their fellow citizens remains opposed to these doctrines, experience shows that many of them, sooner or later, manage to come into contact with German organizations. In many cases these elements do not hesitate to enlist the help of the Nazis, when they cannot make their ideas triumph through their own endeavors. They even go to the extreme of helping the German when he attacks their own country. No act of treachery is too base for these misguided zealots, who would rather see their country enslaved than help in defending it against aggression on the part of the adherents of their cherished faith.

Such people—a free citizen of Holland is forced to admit with shame—were to be found in the Netherlands in such numbers that when the hour of trial came they proved to be a real danger. It was not that they formed so large a section of the community as to have any considerable influence on the public affairs of Holland in times of peace: they were only very feebly represented in Parliament and in the provincial and municipal councils. Nevertheless, when the invader came, their number proved to be such that, when added to the Germans in the country helping the assailants, they created grave difficulties for the loyal citizens and, more especially, for the armed forces. They disposed of large quantities of arms which had lain hidden in different places; one large depot was found at the house of the old Chancellor of the German Legation.

The ways in which these people acted were numerous: at night they guided airplanes by flashing signals or by firing colored rockets; during the daytime, they created confusion by spreading false rumors. Worse still, in order to unnerve the population, they shot from roofs and windows at soldiers and even at civilians passing by. Some houses which they had occupied were regular little fortresses; and in a few cases of this kind at The Hague, artillery had to be brought into action in the streets in order to destroy these strongholds. Serious as all this was, it should be remarked that some grossly exaggerated stories have been circulating in this respect—possibly as a part of the campaign of spreading false rumors. It is not true, for instance, that fifth columnists captured an armored car, in which they drove through the city, shooting at random and killing and wounding many of their fellow citizens. But the fact remains that in several streets in The Hague and Rotterdam these demented fanatics, in some cases helped by their children, built barricades, from behind which they shot at anyone who came in sight. The sternest action was taken to subdue this menace from within, and it may be said that after the second day of war their activity had been reduced to almost nil. Yet now and then, shots were fired from various places in many towns, keeping the citizens in a constant state of unrest and agitation.

Parachutists, troop-carrying airplanes, and fifth columnists gave the reserve troops of the army so much to do that they were prevented from coming to the aid of the front-line troops. Everybody wearing military uniform was thrown into action, even the troops in depot who had joined the army only five weeks earlier and were still in the initial stage of military training. These young soldiers were amazing in their élan. The German High Command, in their instructions which had fallen into Dutch hands, spoke scathingly of these men as "useless and undisciplined." When put to the test, however, they fought with such courage and fury against the German air-borne troops, that they were the primary cause of the failure of the German action against the seat of the Government. For this audacious attempt had missed its object: the parachutists were mopped up, the troops landed from the air never reached The Hague, thanks also to the bravery of a number of youths whose patriotic fervor more than made up for whatever they might lack in military experience.

The Dutch army had been trained and equipped for purposes of defense rather than of attack. As a consequence of the German invasion from the air, however, our soldiers were confronted with the necessity of launching attacks in our difficult flat terrain, a task our High Command had always hoped would fall to the lot of the enemy to attempt.

The German Staff had counted on taking The Hague on the first day. But Dutch resistance proved to be far greater than was expected, and German reinforcements were summoned. Early in the afternoon of the 10th, fresh waves of parachutists descended around The Hague, and troop-carrying aircraft began to land along the coast. At once the Dutch navy took its chance. Gunfire from our warships destroyed these new invaders almost as soon as they landed, so that this fresh menace also came to nothing. The Germans—be it said in honor of the Dutch forces which fought so valiantly that day—had been thwarted in the execution of their plans. When their instructions were found on the body of General von Sponeck, the extent to which the enemy's advance had been delayed became fully apparent.

In other respects also, these papers were extremely interesting, since they showed the thoroughness with which Germany prepares her operations. They included a very accurate list of addresses where stocks of uniforms and arms for the use of the Germans had been concealed, of places where information could be obtained, of inhabitants of The Hague who were to be arrested without delay. Everything was illustrated by very good maps and sketches. Among those who were to be taken prisoner were a number of officers serving on the General Staff of the Dutch Army; they were apparently to receive some form of treatment different from that of ordinary prisoners of war. If that was not the plan, it is difficult to see why they were specially mentioned: what that treatment was to be is not hard to guess. Measures were taken, when this became known, to send all these officers out of the country before it was too late.

Such parachutist troops around The Hague as had been able to escape death or capture the first day, received reinforcements during the following night and in the early morning of May 11th, so that large numbers of Dutch troops again had to be employed to round them up, which again was accomplished successfully. In Rotterdam, the result of the struggle was less favorable. These Dutch troops, supported by small naval craft, stormed the bridges across the Meuse, but were driven off when fresh German troops were landed in great numbers from the air on the nearby landing field of Waalhaven. It became increasingly important to make this airdrome unfit for further use. Two men-of-war were therefore sent to Rotterdam; at the same time, the British Royal Air Force was asked to subject the airdrome to an intense bombardment, which it did on three successive nights. The army was unable to send extra artillery to Rotterdam, as all available guns were in use elsewhere. One of the warships therefore shelled the airdrome, without support from the second vessel which had been stopped further down the river by magnetic mines. *H.M.S. van Galen*, while doing admirable work, at once became the target of innumerable enemy bombers. Thirty-one attacks by dive bombers were successfully repulsed before the ship received a direct hit and had to be abandoned in a sinking condition. The crew at once continued their activities on land, by taking part in the struggle going on in the town of Rotterdam itself, where at that moment the despicable fifth columnists were particularly troublesome. Some British destroyers which had arrived at the mouth of the river were advised not to proceed further because of magnetic mines.

The bitterest struggle of all was fought for the Waalhaven airdrome. Especially in the beginning the field constantly changed hands. More than once it was regained by the Dutch, at the cost of hundreds of lives, only to be retaken by fresh German contingents arriving from the south. After the action of *H.M.S. van Galen* and the nightly bombing attacks of the Royal Air Force had made the airdrome unfit for use, the Germans started landing their aircraft on the parking grounds of a nearby football stadium. The situation soon became even more serious. From a ship flying the Swedish flag, which had been lying in Rotterdam harbor for some time, the Germans were seen to fetch supplies of guns and ammunition which apparently lay hidden beneath its cargo; soon a lively artillery duel was going on across the river between these guns and such artillery as the Dutch had available there—a spot where no one, except the Germans, had even anticipated fighting of this kind.

Finally, when after more than four days neither The Hague nor Rotterdam had been captured, the Germans did a monstrous thing. They resorted to a merciless bombardment on a colossal scale of the open town of Rotterdam, where the Dutch had never dreamt of fighting, and where fighting had only taken place because the Germans attacked the city. This bombardment was one of the worst crimes of military history. Two groups, each of 27 airplanes, systematically bombed the center of the town with heavy high-explosive and incendiary bombs, leaving not a house intact, scarcely a soul alive. Thirty thousand innocent victims, among whom were scarcely any soldiers, perished during the half hour this loathsome raid lasted—old men, young men, women, and innumerable children. Who, in the face of such facts, is there to speak of "Deutsche Ehre, " of "Deutsche Treue"? There is every reason to put this question—it is by no means a mere rhetorical one.

At 10.30 A. M. of that fateful day, the Commander of the troops which had come to Rotterdam to resist the German attack on that otherwise undefended city received an ultimatum in writing to cease fire forthwith, failing which the severest measures would be taken against the town. A reply was demanded within two hours. The document was unsigned. Fearing that it might be a ruse of some sort the Dutch Commander received orders from headquarters to reply that a demand of this kind could only be examined if it were duly signed by a qualified officer. This reply was handed to the Germans at 12.15—a quarter of an hour before the expiration of the time stated in the unsigned document. More than an hour later, at 1.20 P. M., a fresh ultimatum arrived, this time duly signed. It gave another three hours' delay. At 1.22, the first squadron of German bombers approached the city. The Germans twice caused a red flare to be fired, which meant, according to the declarations they made later, that the bombardment was not then to take place. But if this meant anything at all, it did not prevent the bombardment from being executed at once with the utmost brutality. It is not too much to say that, even if this was not bad faith but culpable negligence, culpable negligence of such magnitude reflects most seriously on the honor and trustworthiness of the German command. Errors of this scope, resulting in the wiping out of thirty thousand human beings most of whom were civilians, are unpardonable. An army like that of the Germans, priding itself on its sense of organization, ought to feel deeply humiliated by such a ghastly event.

The Germans tried to put the blame on someone else. First they singled out for censure the Commander of the Dutch troops then in Rotterdam. The facts just stated prove the complete innocence of this officer. Later, German propaganda knew no better than to say that, when all was said and done, the British were to blame!

All the Germans could subsequently do was to try to minimize in their broadcasts the importance of the havoc they had perpetrated; but photographs taken by the British Royal Air Force a few days after the bombardment had taken place speak a language which Dr. Goebbels and his propaganda cannot silence. Conditions in Rotterdam cried to Heaven. Owing to the bombardment, the water supply was cut off and the inhabitants had to be warned to drink only boiled water, for fear of a typhoid epidemic breaking out. Every day the Dutch radio issued SOS messages for food, mattresses, and clothing on behalf of the hapless survivors of German brutality. The new Central Post Office, the Stock Exchange, part of the Town Hall, innumerable other public and private buildings were a shapeless mass of smoking ruins, under which the innocent victims lay buried. Nobody who has known this prosperous, industrious city, where commerce and trade were the chief activities and where civic devotion was always out to further public welfare, can suppress a feeling of fury and disgust when thinking that in this enlightened twentieth century there is a nation always ready to boast of its attainments, yet at the same time capable of such crimes. But, of course, it was against the German will. "Wir haben dies nicht gewollt," Herr von Ribbentrop had said in his memorandum. The Dutch only were to blame. What business had they to fight? What gave them the insolent temerity to resist Germany's aggression?

The Dutch army meanwhile was doing all it could to stem the tide of the German advance in the north and east of the country. No sooner had the first German units crossed the frontier in the early morning hours in the extreme north, than the installations of Delfzijl harbor were destroyed by the Dutch so that they could be of no use to the enemy. In these regions, which because of the flat and open nature of the terrain do not lend themselves to defensive action, our troops had to be content with retarding the enemy's movements. In the night between the 10th and 11th of May, the Zuyderzee dyke enabled our troops to reach positions they could hold. These were promptly attacked by the Germans the next day. A remarkable battle was fought by the Dutch at Kornwerderzand. Here it was proved that even mastery in the air is of no avail against troops occupying shelters protected by concrete of sufficient thickness. After a prolonged preparation by artillery from the air, the invading infantry attempted to storm the position. Skillful use of automatic weapons by the defenders reduced the attempt to complete failure. Next day, a fresh attack was launched, which was likewise repulsed. One of the vessels of the Royal Navy, operating from a position some miles away as the shallow water prevented it from drawing near, gave valuable support to the land forces with its artillery, directed by telephone from the casemates to the naval staff and from there by radio to the ship. A German battery, located at the eastern extremity of the causeway, eleven miles from the place from which the warship was shelling it, was completely silenced within a short time. Visibility was very slight near the vessel's anchorage; the German air force was unable to discover the gun boat and the invader must have been greatly puzzled to know who was destroying his batteries.

The Zuyderzee dyke, that masterpiece of Dutch engineering, was never taken by the enemy.

When the dyke proved too much for the German army to force, German detachments of all sizes appeared on the eastern shores of the Zuyderzee, and began to make preparations for crossing it to the provinces of Holland. Since there were no more Dutch troops available for the northern part of those provinces, steps were taken to reinforce without delay the flotilla operating on the Zuyderzee. Torpedo boats, gunboats, and mine-sweepers were hurriedly sent, together with a number of armed river craft and motorboats provided with heavy machine guns. These units were soon reinforced by French and British motor torpedo boats, which arrived in the night between the 12th and 13th of May. The German air force was a harassing factor in this action, sinking two gunboats, one of which succeeded in reaching the ancient port of Enkhuizen where it continued firing by way of harbor battery. In spite of losses, however, the German attempts at crossing the Zuyderzee remained unsuccessful. This was the first battle to be fought on the Zuyderzee since 1578, when the Dutch had a naval engagement with the Spaniards on these inland waters. After three and a half centuries of peace, it was the Germans who made them once again the scene of armed conflict.

In the south, where the Germans were out to use Dutch territory for their onslaught upon France through Belgium, our troops found themselves confronted with vastly superior forces. The German air force, which had complete mastery in the air, effectively covered the advance of the armored and motorized units. No sooner was this support temporarily absent, however, and the German infantry without the protection of armored vehicles and planes, than the Dutch army inflicted heavy losses on the enemy. The crossing of the canal connecting the rivers Meuse and Waal, and of the Meuse itself, cost the Germans a heavy toll of life before the Dutch automatic weapons contesting these crossings could be silenced.

Unfortunately, the aggressor proved too powerful. His advance could not be checked. French troops arrived, but they, too had to retreat owing to German pressure. Limburg and the greater part of the province of Brabant had to be abandoned. The blowing up of a German armored train near the village of Mill deserves special mention. This train, one of the four armored trains which advanced into Holland and which were all wiped out, crossed the Meuse at an early hour on Friday, before the bridge over which it passed could be destroyed by our troops. Near Mill, this fortress on wheels was brought to a standstill and destroyed by the second regiment of Field Artillery in collaboration with formations of motorized cavalry. Another armored train met its fate when it crossed a bridge near Venlo at the very moment it was blown up;

bridge and train crashed into the swirling waters of the Meuse.

Once the Germans were master in the greater part of Brabant they were in a position to pour their troops at will into the province of Holland. They were now no longer solely dependent on air-borne troops in the country's center. Yet, although the battle was a desperate one, the Dutch put up a very gallant struggle in defense of the heart of their land, so much so that, as we have already seen, the enemy took recourse to the most inhuman means in order to capture Rotterdam. The German army, meanwhile, after crossing the frontier along its whole length on the very first day of their attack, advanced steadily not only in the extreme north and in the southern section of the frontier, but also in its middle regions. There, their onrush was first retarded by our frontier troops, and later, when these had been withdrawn according to plan, by the fortified banks of the river Yssel, which caused them further delay. In spite of their overwhelming power and motorized columns, it took the Germans three full days to cover the distance of roughly fifty miles between the frontier and the outposts of the main lines of our defenses, which were covered by a continuous broad belt of inundated territory. The water, so often our enemy, had this time been harnessed to render us great services.

On these lines the Germans launched a fierce attack; innumerable low-flying aircraft supported the assault on the defenders, followed by flame-throwing tanks and others. The lines held, except in one sector; before, however, the enemy could exploit this advantage, the Dutch army counterattacked, driving the Germans completely out of the positions they had just occupied at great cost to themselves. Next day the Germans renewed their attack on a still larger sector. Against overwhelming forces and superior equipment, this main line of resistance could be held no longer. The Dutch army withdrew to new positions which had been carefully prepared in advance, again protected by inundations.

Were it not that our reserves had been exhausted by the incessant fighting in the heart of the country since the first hours of war, these troops would now have proved invaluable. They could—and were meant to—have occupied these last lines of resistance, letting through the troops retreating from the east while shielding them, and allowing them to reorganize themselves for further action. As it was, the withdrawing troops had to retreat and at the same time occupy the new lines, thereby shouldering the whole burden of the final engagement. Is it to be wondered at that in those circumstances they were unable to hold their own? Battered in the east, and with a wide breach in the south, the extensive fortified area of Holland could finally be held no longer.

This development had been foreseen in London, where the Queen had arrived the evening before. I had a long conversation with Her Majesty in the apartments at Buckingham Palace which the King had placed at her disposal.

It was an hour of deep and real sorrow. Our troops had put up a very brave stand against overwhelming odds. They had been confronted not only with all the refinements of modern war technique developed to a degree unparalleled in history, but by every form of treachery and deceit, from without and from within. Rotterdam had, in part, been wiped from the earth. The beautiful old town of Utrecht was threatened by the enemy with a similar fate. Even then, it had been agreed not to give up further resistance. The Queen had explained the situation to the King of England; it was decided that I was to do the same with regard to the British military authorities, while Her Majesty addressed a telegram to the President of the French Republic. The position was the following: either the Allies were to send adequate assistance without delay, and in that case we would fight on, or, if such adequate assistance could not be sent, the Dutch military commanders were to be empowered to act as they judged best, weighing the results that might be expected from further resistance, against the suffering this must inevitably cause to the civilian population of the densely populated country. It was past midnight when I reached the British High Command. There, it was considered that this was a perfectly fair statement to make in our predicament. But no help of any real importance could be promised.

I know that there have been complaints in the Netherlands to the effect that we obtained little help from our

Allies. It may be that more help had been expected, but I, for my part, have the absolute conviction that our Allies, both British and French, did what they could. It was our common misfortune that they had no more resources available. Twice I had a discussion on the subject with the British Prime Minister, Mr. Churchill. He was completely frank, and various measures of assistance were at once taken, but they could not be extensive enough to save the situation. In so far as there was any comfort to be derived from these discussions, it was that they gave me the certainty that, even if we could have had any prearranged plans with the Allies for common defense in the case of a German attack, we would have obtained no more help than we obtained now. No more was available. That is the best answer to give to those superficial critics of our policy of neutrality, who are always prone to say: "If only you had had the wisdom to reverse your attitude before it was too late."

When, only a few weeks later, the French Command had to consider whether or no they were to defend Paris, they took the view that no valuable strategic result justified the sacrifice of that city. The Dutch Command in the fortified area of Holland took the same view when the Germans had succeeded in making wide breaches in its eastern and southern defenses. Combat to the last man would certainly have inflicted serious losses on the enemy, but, in view of his enormous superiority in arms and in men, neither our cause nor that of our Allies could have gained by such prolongation of resistance. At the same time there is no doubt, especially with a foe applying German methods, that the whole of that once flourishing country with its many beautiful old cities, great art treasures, historic monuments and smiling countryside, would have been methodically devastated and a considerable part of its population wiped out, as had happened in Rotterdam.

In those circumstances, General Winkelman, in whose hands the decision lay, resolved to give the order to cease fire. The Cabinet had left the previous day and followed the Queen to England. It was a bitter moment for the gallant soldier who had so ably conducted the operations and who, were it not that the presence of millions of noncombatants had forced him to decide otherwise, would beyond doubt have infinitely preferred to fight until the last.

In a few quarters, ignorant people have flippantly stated that the Netherlands Commander in Chief "had lost his nerve." It would be difficult to find a more gross injustice against a man whose steadfastness, courage, and fighting spirit have stood the most crucial test. I can only express the greatest respect for a General who prefers to risk and to face hasty, unfounded, and uncharitable criticism on the part of the uninformed public rather than to subject his countrymen, for no useful purpose, to the horrors of further mass slaughter, with, as the only possible favorable result, still more glory added to that already achieved by our army against the most infernal war machine of all times.

The Netherlands Government has never capitulated. Although the European part of the Kingdom is under German occupation, the overseas territories are free. The Kingdom of the Netherlands, constitutionally a unit, continues to have all a State must have in order to be called a State: it has territory, it has a population, it has a legitimate Government—the Queen and Dynasty are safe. That Government is now continuing the struggle with all the means at its disposal, including the Royal Navy, which is at present operating in conjunction with the Allied forces. Germany's power over the European part of the Netherlands is based merely on force, and she has not acquired that measure of right and title which an act of submission by the legitimate Government might have given her.

The army in the provinces of Holland had been forced to capitulate; the army in the province of Zeeland continued the struggle. In this island province, the fighting lasted for several more days. There, French troops and the British navy were able to render valuable assistance, which they did to the limits of their power. The beautiful ancient Town Hall of Middelburg, a gem of sixteenth-century Dutch architecture, as well as the old Abbey, so often the delight of overseas visitors, were both reduced to ruins.

Many a tale could be told of the courage and determination shown by the defenders of the southwest corner of Holland, greatly heartened by the presence of Prince Bernhard, who returned from taking his family to England in order to be with the army. They gallantly struggled on until the last. There were the pupils of an army flying school, who, when the situation seemed desperate, took off, although they had barely mastered the art of flying, in their instruction planes, landing them safely in French airports. There was the young lieutenant who, ordered in the midst of a bombardment to rescue the available cash from the Netherlands Bank at Middelburg, forced the front door "by leaning against it," as he put it, collected a large sum of money from the shivering and protesting Manager, who had taken refuge in the strongroom, and brought it safely to Paris after a narrow escape from the enemy, then hardly two miles away. These episodes, and so many others, recede into the background of that grim scene where the last act of the Dutch tragedy was coming to a close. Before the month of May was at an end, Zeeland, and thereby the whole country, was under German occupation.

So the curtain closes on a country which, within five days, was reduced from a high degree of prosperity to a state of semiruin, where hungry Germans have bought everything—if an exchange of valuable goods for German "Kassenscheine" of doubtful value deserves the name of buying. Worse still, in that country where public health was at a very high standard, and where the mortality rate was the lowest in Europe, the hospitals are now packed with wounded, while innumerable families mourn their dead. The Dutch army lost thousands of its young men. The toll taken of some regiments attained a very high figure: let us remember here with deep respect our gallant Grenadiers who, after storming two airdromes in one day, had lost eighty percent of their manpower. But then this is clear to all the world: "Wir haben es nicht gewollt," said Herr von Ribbentrop.

Before ending this chapter, a point of capital importance must be mentioned. It is necessary to define exactly the position of the Netherlands, after fighting on land had come to an end. When war began for the Netherlands, the country was completely free, unfettered by any arrangement with any power, to resist as long as it saw fit. It resisted to the utmost. It did not give in, even when it was clear that little Allied help was forthcoming and that there was no chance of stemming the invasion. At any time during the five days of the struggle, the Dutch would have been free to bargain for some humiliating armistice. But although they are said to be good bargainers in matters of commerce, they showed disdain for negotiation when the country's highest interests were at stake. They fought until further fighting was impossible; the honor of the country was saved. Glory has been added to the ancient war records of Holland. The Government preferred seeing the country wholly occupied by the enemy to accepting some dishonorable arrangement, under which they would have been reduced to the state of vassal with their own signature at the bottom of the document. Suffering violence and agreeing to suffer it are to the Dutch mind two very different things. How and when Holland will rise again as a free country, nobody knows. But that one day it will recover its secular freedom is an article of faith for all.

Dynasty and Government

WHEN the German attack began in the early morning of May 10th, the Queen was at the Huis ten Bosch, her quaint old palace near The Hague with its souvenirs of William and Mary and so many other Stadholders and Kings and Queens of the House of Orange. The first attack from the air opened at about 4 o'clock, and it was obvious at once that the Royal Palace was one of the principal targets. Wave after wave of bombers came over. During the entire forenoon of the first day the Queen was forced to take refuge in her bomb-proof shelter. Messengers came and went with the latest news from the front and from the cities. As the attack developed, it became clear that the Huis ten Bosch was no longer sufficiently safe. Parachute troops were landing in the neighborhood in considerable numbers. The surrounding woods made it easy for them to conceal themselves, and the Palace Guards could be taken by surprise. Beyond the woods lay flat fields—ideal landing grounds for troop-carrying planes. Some parachutists actually landed in the garden of the Royal Palace, and were promptly shot down by the Guards. But the situation was becoming very dangerous and a move was imperative.

Three miles away, in the center of the town, stood the

Noordeinde Palace. This was considered to be safer, and the Royal party set out late in the afternoon. As a preliminary, the woods had been cleared of snipers, and once in town the Queen's escort was able to prevent anybody from shooting from roofs and windows. But hardly were the Queen and her Family installed in their new sanctuary when shots rang out from houses surrounding the Palace gardens. The treacherous fifth column was in action. At once the Queen's Guards set out to clear the neighborhood. Some Germans and a few Dutch were caught, while a few managed to get away. Prince Bernhard himself took an active part in getting rid of these pests. During the whole morning he had hunted parachutists and machine-gunned low-flying planes at the Huis ten Bosch. Now, he set up a machine gun on the roof of the Palace and successfully kept up a heavy fire against any snipers he could detect.

The Queen, with Princess Juliana and her two children, found protection in the heavily armored shelter in the Noordeinde Palace. In this narrow steel and concrete space they were forced to spend three days and two nights, anxiously following the developments of the struggle and remaining in constant touch with the Cabinet and the High Command. As early as Friday, May 10th, it had become clear that the Germans, as in Norway, were hunting the Royal Family, without making even the slightest endeavor to spare their lives.

Wilhelmina Helena Paulina Maria Queen of the Netherlands, Princess of the ancient House of Orange-Nassau, Duchess of Mecklenburg, was born in 1880. When she was ten years old she succeeded her father, the late King William III. As she was then a minor, a regency was proclaimed lasting until her eighteenth birthday, when, under the Constitution of the Netherlands, she attained her majority. Her mother, the Dowager Queen Emma, was Regent for her daughter. Until and after her death in 1934 that gracious and wise royal lady held a special place in the devoted affection of her daughter's subjects. She gave all her attention to preparing the young Queen for her great task of ruling the Netherlands and their vast overseas territories and of continuing the high traditions of impartiality, political insight, and selfless care for the public weal which have given the monarchy under the House of Orange-Nassau a place in the eyes of the nation which no other form of Government could hold.

Ever since 1898, the Queen has ruled her country in her own name. It has become a great reign, a period of peaceful development, bringing extensive social reforms, improved education and increasing general prosperity. The population grew steadily. In the Dutch East Indies, her beneficent rule brought final pacification to the most remote islands. A public welfare policy has been inaugurated there which has proved eminently successful. Political reforms have been introduced in a progressive spirit. It has always been Dutch policy to coöperate closely with the native population in questions of administration.

Under Her Majesty's wise guidance this responsibility on the part of the native element has been considerably increased. Representative institutions have been organized and encouraged in villages, districts, provinces, as well as with regard to the affairs of the territory as a whole. Dutch Colonial administration can bear comparison with any in the world.

In 1901, the Queen married Duke Henry of Mecklenburg-Schwerin. When, eight years later, a Princess was born to them the country's jubilations knew no bounds. The future of the Dynasty, one of the pillars of the state, seemed assured, and when the little Princess, who has always enjoyed great popularity, was herself married to Prince Bernhard of Lippe-Biesterfeld, the event was celebrated with unbounded joy by every one of the Queen's loyal subjects. Renewed manifestations of the happiness the whole nation felt greeted the birth of the Queen's two grandchildren: Princess Beatrix, now two and a half years old, and the little Princess born a month before the outbreak of war, to whom her parents, as an invocation of peace, gave the name of Irene.

Royal simplicity characterizes the Queen. Her innumerable duties she fulfills with the greatest devotion, conferring with her ministers, studying state papers, visiting military and naval establishments, attending to works of charity, and all those many interests which as a true mother of her country she has at heart. Profoundly religious, Her Majesty has always taken an active interest in missionary work, and of later years her stimulating efforts to contribute to the moral rearmament of her country have shown in yet another way her deep interest in things spiritual. Until her sixtieth year, the Queen never declared war on any state, nor has any other state during that period resorted to armed force against the Netherlands. Because of the conservative and stable policy described earlier in this book, the country gave offense to no one and lived in friendship and peace with all. How Germany brought this blessed period to an end we have seen.

The Queen left nothing undone to prevent war. All her thoughts and her energies were directed towards this end. When, late in August, the representatives of the smaller European states met in Brussels to make an urgent appeal to their more powerful neighbors to preserve peace, it was largely thanks to the warm-hearted support the Queen so fully gave in this matter to the King of the Belgians. Even at the last hour, Her Majesty offered her good offices at The Hague to the prospective belligerents, while King Leopold, acting in conjunction with her, did the same at Brussels. During Finland's grim struggle with the Russian hordes, the Queen generously contributed towards succoring the civilian population in the gallant republic. In November, 1939, she and King Leopold once more assured the belligerents of their readiness to bring them together if it were thought that the two friendly sovereigns could usefully act as intermediaries.

All this, and a great deal more of which the public will never know, was done by Her Majesty in order to ward off from her country as well as from others the evil of war. She worked untiringly. All news, good or bad, was by her own order at once communicated to her. It made no difference whether it came at midday or in the small hours of the morning. A quick decision might be essential. No chance that might help to stop the continuing crisis must be missed. The Queen was indefatigable. In all weathers she visited and inspected army and navy posts along the coasts and the frontiers. The one relaxation and the bright spot in these months of vigilant toil were the short hours devoted to her children and grandchildren.

Everybody who had the honor of coming into contact with Her Majesty during that time, knew that if the worst were to happen the Queen would not fail to be a great source of strength to her people and to all those around her; and when the worst did happen, their anticipations were fully realized.

In order to safeguard the future of the Dynasty so essential in the public affairs of the Netherlands, it was decided to move the Princess and her children to England where their safety could be assured. The Queen insisted that the Prince should accompany his wife, but he was to return to Holland as soon as possible in order to resume his duties as Her Majesty's Aide-de-Camp. A first attempt at making the journey was undertaken on Friday evening. Princess Juliana and the children were already in the motor car which was to take them to the coast when a message came that the journey was impossible: parachutists and air-borne troops were still at large, shooting from behind hedges and dykes at anybody in sight. Although a great number had been wiped out during the daytime, those that remained were still too numerous for the Princess and her party to travel in safety. The next day, after fresh German troops had landed in the dunes, fields, and woods around The Hague, the journey still was considered too unsafe. At last, after another day and night in the small shelter, the country had been cleared to such an extent that an attempt could be made. To use an armored car as a conveyance was out of the question. There was far too little room for the Royal party. Someone made the fortunate suggestion of using an armored motor car belonging to the Netherlands Bank which, although not shell proof, afforded reasonable protection against machine-gun bullets. Thirty marines accompanied the party, heavily armed with automatic weapons; they left The Hague towards 8 o'clock on Sunday evening, and drove at great speed to the harbor of Ymuiden, where the British destroyer *Codrington* under Commander Creasy lay waiting. All went well until the party was about to board the warship; then, suddenly, in the waning light of the long summer's evening, a German airplane appeared overhead. The pilot had discovered the destroyer and dived to attack. All were holding their breath. Was he going to machine-gun the Royal travelers?

He skimmed over them without shooting, and proceeded to bomb the warship. The first bomb missed the destroyer, and once again the plane climbed back to renew the attack. This time a magnetic mine was dropped in front of the vessel. In the narrow harbor entrance, this would have prevented it from putting out to sea, had not a miracle happened. The parachute attached to the mine failed to open, and as a result the mine hit the water's surface with such violence that it exploded at once. Apart from wounding a man on the quayside, so far as could be seen, no further damage was done, and Commander Creasy was able to put to sea. An accompanying vessel was shortly afterwards attacked by a group of German dive bombers, without success. After that, all went smoothly. Next morning the Princess and her children, accompanied by the Prince, arrived safely in an English port. The Dynasty was safe: the joy everybody felt when it was realized that the Germans had not succeeded in capturing these members of the House of Orange was immense throughout the country. The young Princesses stood the journey very well, the elder even enjoying its novelty; Princess Juliana showed great coolness and courage in these hours of trial, and Prince Bernhard gave proof of considerable resource.

While the Prince was completing arrangements for returning to Holland, news was received in London that the Queen was on her way to Great Britain. It was only after Her Majesty's arrival that we learned the reasons which had made her take this momentous decision. The military situation in Holland had gone from bad to worse, in spite of the gallant fight of the Dutch soldiers, inspired by the thought of defending their country and all it stands for. On Monday morning, May 13th, the Commander in Chief informed the Queen and her Government that he could no longer assume responsibility for their safety. The Germans were threatening to bomb Rotterdam (which they did with terrible results the afternoon of the next day) and pressure on the Dutch lines was such that it appeared more than doubtful whether they could be held much longer. The Queen decided that in no case would she render the Germans the service of allowing herself to be captured. Since The Hague became increasingly unsafe, it was thought best to proceed to the southwest corner of the country, to the mainland of Zeeland. The journey by land was out of the question. All Dutch men-of-war were heavily engaged in action with the enemy, so a British warship was placed at the Queen's disposal. It was a fine day and, were it not that the vessel had to steer a zigzag course against possible submarine attacks, it would have been a smooth journey. From time to time German planes were sighted, though they did not attack. But suddenly a disturbing message reached the warship. The little Zeeland harbor of Breskens, where Her Majesty was to disembark, was being heavily bombarded from the air. Whether the enemy had news of the Queen's departure and destination will probably always remain a secret. The fact remains that until then Breskens had been untouched. There was no town of importance, nor any military objective in the neighborhood. The conclusion seems obvious: it was a trap. The Germans hoped to destroy at Breskens what they had failed to capture at The Hague.

Her Majesty resolved not to play into their hands. Scarcely had the wireless message been received than the destroyer's bell signals rang out. Heavily she heeled over, altering her course westward—to England. The low dunes along the Zeeland coast faded slowly below the horizon, and as the late afternoon light deepened, the coast of England rose ahead. The destroyer stood in for an English port, with the Queen and her suite quite safe.

Let us place on record here the conspicuous part played by the British Royal Navy in ensuring the safe arrival in England of the Netherlands Royal House. No Dutchman can but feel deep gratitude to these officers and men who, at a time when all our naval units were fully engaged with the enemy, cared for the safety of the Orange Dynasty. They, too, helped in thwarting Herr Hitler's grim purpose and his desperate attempts to capture the Royal Family by parachutists, or to kill them by machine-gunning all places where they resided. Note the striking contrast: on the one hand, persistent efforts to hunt two women of royal birth and two baby princesses, together with their father; on the other, a number of British sailors who, at the peril of their own life, did all in their power to protect a Dynasty which stands for so much that forms part of what most honors our civilization? Once in England, the Queen gave public expression to her feelings of deep appreciation and gratitude.

Queen Wilhelmina's arrival under the spacious roof of murky Liverpool Street Station in London was a scene no one who witnessed it will ever forget. As the train slowly came to a standstill, a number of grim-looking soldiers in Dutch uniform jumped onto the platform. They still were in full battle dress, with rifles and hand grenades, automatic pistols, and the battered steel helmets they were wearing when told to abandon the struggle in order to accompany their Queen. They stood out in strange contrast to the hundreds of peaceful onlookers. A police cordon held back the crowd as King George came forward to welcome the Queen and offer her hospitality. As the two Sovereigns greeted each other, it could clearly be seen that at this historical moment they were not only Sovereigns, but human beings who fully realized the tragedy of the hour. Here was a Queen who, in the course of a long reign, had been so good a ruler of her country that she had won the deeply affectionate respect of two generations. Now, she had been driven from her realm by a ruthless act of aggression on the part of a nation to which she was related by kinship, which she had never harmed in any way. She had always striven to see and acknowledge the good side of the Germans, and to foster good relations. In her sixtieth year, fate decreed that it was to be of no avail. Tired and shocked by what had happened, shaken by all she had gone through the last four days, she stood there, still undaunted and full of purpose, though for the time being an exile in a foreign land. Everybody present realized what this episode meant to her. The crowd cheered, but in their cheers was a note, not only of compassionate sympathy but also of admiration for a great lady, whose courage, though sorely tried, remained so visibly unbroken. Here was a Queen who, it was felt by everybody who saw her then, lived up to the high standards set by her forebears, William the Silent and the Stadholder King, William the Third.

After Queen Elizabeth had greeted her Royal visitor on her arrival at Buckingham Palace, Queen Wilhelmina withdrew to the apartments placed at her disposal and, indefatigable, at once resumed her task. How was resistance to be carried further? What help could be expected from the Allies? Had contact been taken up with France as it had with Great Britain? How was the position to be made clear to the people of the Netherlands and to the world at large? These, and many others, were the problems which were at once eagerly discussed. More than one important decision was taken and carried into effect. Only at midnight of that momentous and tragic day did the Queen at last retire to rest.

The next day, a Royal Proclamation was issued by Her Majesty to her people. At that time, direct communication by telephone with Holland had been cut off; but it still proved possible to speak with those at The Hague by the use of the wireless telephone via New York. So it happened that Queen Wilhelmina's proclamation was flashed to her subjects by way of the United States of America.

This proclamation was one of two documents issued by the Queen during her first days in London, which should be rescued from oblivion. The second was a statement the Queen released for publication a few days later. In her proclamation, Her Majesty exhorted her people not to lose heart, and to remember past afflictions from which the country had always triumphantly arisen. In the article released for publication, Queen Wilhelmina gave to all the world the reasons which moved her to leave her country. Any comment on these documents would detract from their value rather than enhance it; therefore they are quoted here in full.

PROCLAMATION

BY THE QUEEN OF THE NETHERLANDS

TO HER PEOPLE, DATED FROM LONDON,

MAY 13TH, 1940

"After it had become absolutely certain that We and Our Ministers could no longer continue freely to exercise state authority in the Netherlands, the hard, but necessary, decision had to be taken of removing the seat of Government abroad for as long as will prove inevitable, with the intention of returning immediately to the Netherlands as soon as this is at all possible.

"The Government is at present in England. As a Government it does not wish to capitulate. Thereby the Netherlands territories which remain in Dutch hands, in Europe as well as in the East and West Indies, continue to be a sovereign state, which will continue to raise its voice and to assert its position, especially in the joint deliberations of the Allies, as a fully recognized member of the community of states.

"The military authorities, and in the highest instance the Commander in Chief of the Naval and Land forces, will from now on judge what measures are necessary and justifiable from a military point of view.

"Where the invader is in power, the local civil authorities must continue to take those measures which may be useful in the interests of the population. They should in the first place contribute towards preserving law and order.

"Our heart goes out to our compatriots, who will pass through hard times in our country. But the time will come when the Netherlands, with God's help, will regain their European territory. Remember catastrophes in former centuries, and the resurrection of the Netherlands which followed. Thus it will also be this time.

"Let no one despair. Let everybody do his utmost in the well-understood interests of the country. We do Ours.

"*Long live the Netherlands!*"

In those words Queen Wilhelmina took leave, for a period unknown, of her people. When she addressed the whole world to make clear her reasons for leaving Holland, this was her message:

"At this immensely grave moment in the history of mankind black, silent night has settled on yet another corner of this earth.

"Over free Holland the lights have gone out, the wheels of industry and the ploughs of the field that worked only for the happiness of a peace-loving people have come to a dead stop or are turned to the grisly uses of a death-bringing conqueror; the voices of freedom, charity, tolerance, and religion have been stilled.

"Where only two weeks ago there was a free nation of men and women brought up in the cherished traditions of Christian civilization, a nation which itself has been the historical fountain of many values and ideals honored by all men of good will, there are now desolation and the stillness of death, broken only by the bitter weeping of those who have survived the extinction of their relatives and the brutal suppression of their rights and liberties.

"Only hope still lives among the smoking ruins, the hope and faith of a God-fearing people which no human power, however evil, can extinguish—faith in the all-conquering might of Divine justice, faith nourished by the proud memories of earlier ordeals manfully borne and in the end successfully overcome, faith anchored to the unshakable belief that such injustice as the people of Holland have suffered cannot endure.

"But while the unhappy people of Holland still have their faith in the ultimate and inevitable deliverance to cling to, it is of all faiths the most difficult to nourish and to keep alive. For theirs must be a silent hope and a silent faith. Not for them the solace of a faith openly professed, not for them the soul-strengthening comfort of a hope shared and proclaimed in open association.

"Oppressed, threatened, watched on every side by a Power that would tear out all hope from the soul of man, they can but pray in the silence of their heavy hearts. Their voice, the voice that through the centuries has helped to spread the gospel of Christianity, of freedom, of tolerance, of enterprise and thought of human dignity, of all the things that make man worthy of his sojourn on earth, has been taken away from them.

"So it was four centuries ago when religious freedom was at stake. The world knows how the people of Holland then regained their voice. Thus it will be again. But until the jubilation of the new dawn they are not spared even this last bitterness of having to keep their flame of hope alive in the deadly silence of a night whence no voice, no ray of light shall come.

"It is because Holland's voice must not, nay may not be allowed to remain strangled in these days of fearful trial for my people that I have taken the supreme decision to transfer the symbol of My Nation, as it is embodied in

My Person and My Government, where it can continue to function as a living and a vocal force.

"At this time of universal suffering I will not speak of the racking heart-searchings which the taking of this decision has cost one who, only little more than a year ago, was stirred to her very depths by the generous devotion of a warm-hearted people celebrating the jubilee of a Queen and a woman who for forty years has tried to serve Her Nation, as she tried to serve it on that day of fateful decisions and will try to serve it to her last breath.

"I will speak only of the reasons that finally moved me to decide as I did. For there were cold and weighty reasons militating against the natural sentiment that prompted me and my family to stay and suffer what my unhappy people were called upon to suffer.

"Plans found on the invader on the first day of his wanton assault, confirmed by the action of his air-borne troops, soon made it clear that his first objective was to capture the Royal Family and the Government, thus to paralyze the country by depriving it of all leadership and legally constituted authority.

"When, soon afterwards, the likelihood had to be faced that the treacherous methods employed by the enemy would succeed in finally undermining the gallant resistance of the Dutch forces, decision could no longer be postponed.

"If authority, obeying impulsive sentiment, were to stay —for indeed those who, like us, have lived such days know that it is not concern for personal life or liberty which supplies the driving motive—the voice of Holland, the very symbol of Holland, would have vanished from the earth.

"There would be a memory, perhaps quickly fading in these world-shaking times where yesterday's memory is to-day's oblivion. Unrelieved black silence would have settled on that once happy land whose people would not even have the hope-giving thought of a Queen and a Government fighting for their ultimate resurrection, where fighting was still possible.

"But there was more. Holland proper may have been lost for the time being, but when these crucial decisions had to be taken, one province in the south still showed hope of being able to hold out for some time.

"My Navy, with its proud traditions, remained intact, ready to join battle wherever needed, and, most important of all, an Empire scattered over the surface of the globe and counting sixty-five million inhabitants, remained free, part and parcel of that nation of free men that will not and can not perish from the earth.

"Was all this to be cast adrift on a wildly turbulent sea without leadership or authority? Duty, responsibility and far-sighted statesmanship lay elsewhere.

"To keep the voice and the symbol of Holland alive as an inspiration and a rallying-point for those of our Army, our Fleet, and our countless Empire subjects, nay, for Dutch men and women all over the world who will give their all for the resurrection of the dearly beloved Motherland.

"To keep the banner aloft, unseen and yet ever present for those who have lost their voice but not their hope nor their vision.

"To speak for Holland to the world, not of the rightness of its cause, which needs no advocacy in the eyes of honest men, nor of the unspeakable horrors or the infamous tricks inflicted on its gallant army and its innocent population, but of the values, the ideals, the Christian civilization that Holland at the side of its Allies is helping to defend against the onslaught of barbarism.

"To remain true to the motto of the House of Orange, of Holland, of all that immense part of the world that is fighting for what is infinitely more precious than life: *Je maintiendrai*–I shall maintain."

These words speak for themselves. It would be difficult to express more clearly or more cogently why the course the Queen had taken was the only one compatible with the higher and permanent interests of the country. They have a significance for all times. That is why they are reproduced here.

When the Queen arrived in London, the only members of her Cabinet present were the Ministers for Foreign Affairs and Colonies, who had flown to England on the day the invasion began. The next day saw the arrival of their colleagues who had remained in Holland, in spite of the Germans' attempts at capturing them in order to take them to Berlin. Since the battle was in progress day and night, they had had little rest, but their spirit remained undaunted. On Monday evening they, too, were confronted with the anxious question whether they should allow themselves to be taken prisoner, or whether they should leave the country. For this was the alternative; there seemed no prospect of their being allowed to make themselves useful once the Germans had Holland in their grip. They would either be placed in the position of a Schuschnigg, or the Germans might have attempted to use them in order to give their occupation a semblance of legitimacy.

At such grave moments, sentiment tends to engulf reason. And yet, the interests at stake being those not of private persons, nor even of members of the Government, but those of the whole nation, make it imperative that reason should prevail. The Dutch Ministers fully realized this cruel necessity. Not one of them who had remained at The Hague was able to be accompanied by his wife or his children. In the turmoil of street fighting, most of them could not even say good-bye in person to their nearest and dearest; yet they went. A last brief meeting on Dutch soil took place in a fort near the Hook of Holland; a final consultation by telephone with the Commander in Chief, and they were on their way.

They, too, were given a British destroyer to take them to England, where they were to join their Queen. Many attempts were made by enemy aircraft to bomb and sink the vessel; under cover of darkness these last attempts also proved fruitless. Another vessel, which conveyed several members of the diplomatic corps at The Hague, had an even narrower escape. But in the early hours of May 14th, all arrived safely in England.

During the few days that all the members of the Royal Family as well as the Cabinet remained in London, a short ceremony took place on the 31st of May: nine-months old Princess Irene, whose christening had been put off more than once on account of the international situation, was baptized in the private chapel of Buckingham Palace. Queen Elizabeth was the baby's godmother; her godfathers were the highest representatives of the Netherlands army, the navy and the army of the Dutch East Indies. The poignancy of this christening in exile was enhanced by its simplicity: no waving flags, cheering crowds, or gala uniforms. No more than thirty people attended the service, which was held partly in English, with a short address by the Minister of the Dutch Reformed Church in London.

After the death of Lord Tweedsmuir—the gifted Governor General of the Dominion of Canada, the Earl of Athlone was appointed as his successor. Princess Alice, Countess of Athlone, a first cousin of Queen Wilhelmina, had invited Princess Juliana to join them at Ottawa, where the two little girls would be able to live in peace, far from the unrest of Europe—and undisturbed by a repetition of the harrowing experiences through which they had passed. The kind offer was gratefully accepted. A Dutch cruiser took the Princess and her party to Canadian shores, where they were given a warm-hearted welcome.

In all their misfortune the Netherlands were more fortunate than their southern neighbor Belgium, whose King is now a prisoner in the hands of the enemy, while Queen Wilhelmina is in a position to take all decisions necessary in order to work towards the ultimate resurrection of her country as an independent Kingdom. The Belgian Government, as well as the three motherless Royal children, were driven from Belgium to France, from France to Spain, and from Spain to Portugal. The Dutch Government, on the other hand, was at once able to set to work in London to carry on the struggle, to ensure the administration of the Dutch Empire overseas, and to safeguard Dutch interests abroad. In this, they received assistance from numerous Dutch citizens who, in every conceivable way and in many cases at great peril of their lives and personal sacrifice, had managed to find their way to London; some arrived in fishing smacks, others in open boats, others still after incredible peregrinations through Belgium and France, where the war was raging fiercely and crowds of refugees blocked the roads. The offers of service the Government received were far more numerous than they were able to accept. But the all-important affairs of state could be carried on; and, in spite of German ruthlessness, the doors leading to a brighter future have not been closed.

The Future

FOR some time past, the Dutch Government had realized that a European war, if not certain, was extremely probable. Hence the strengthening of the country's defenses; hence, also, the many-sided preparations in the economic sphere. When war broke out, the Netherlands were endowed with complete legislative and administrative machinery to weather the storm. The Government had received far-reaching emergency powers, and the stocks of all important commodities were such that scarcity would only arise in case the country were cut off from overseas markets for some considerable time.

The economic blockade of Germany, put into force by the Allies as soon as war began, made it necessary for Holland to negotiate agreements with France and Great Britain in order to keep the country's stocks at an adequate level. For a variety of reasons, which now have no more than an historic interest, these negotiations were difficult, but they finally resulted in arrangements to which Germany took no exception, however critically that country was wont to look upon every aspect of the policy of neutrality pursued by the Netherlands. As a result, Holland's economic life, although hard hit by the war with its devastating effect on world prosperity, seemed assured of what, taking all the circumstances into account, might be called a tolerable basis. There was enough for everybody; industry could be kept going, be it on a somewhat reduced scale. Rationed necessities were few, fewer than in any of the belligerent countries, and the rations allowed were liberal. Holland still was the land of plenty it had always been.

Hardly were the Germans in occupation, when this happy state of affairs changed as if by magic. The Dutch were forced to accept German currency at a fixed rate, and on this uncertain basis—for, the German Reichsmark not being freely convertible into other currencies, it is difficult to assess its real value—in a very few days Holland had become an empty country. All kinds of commodities were immediately subjected to rationing. Petrol and tires became extremely scarce. But also coffee and tea, which used to be imported into Holland from its own overseas territories and which the Dutch are accustomed to consume in great quantities, became rare. The same applied to shoes and textiles, including all ready-made clothing, of which Germany stood in great need. Bread was soon rationed. This rapid transition to poverty in a country that had always been well-to-do and where the standard of living had been high must have come as a great shock to the population, which had just gone through the agonies of war, and must have damped even the spirits of those who were inclined to be impressed by Nazi successes. Instructions were broadcast how, by drying used tea leaves and adding some fresh ones, the very small monthly allowance could be made to go a little further. This process was also recommended for coffee. Perhaps the only flourishing industry was that of wooden shoes, an article which had come to be used only by farmers and gardeners. Leather being unavailable, they are once more in demand.

The Germans at once proceeded to cut the Dutch people completely off from the outside world. No one was allowed to leave the country without the consent of the now omnipotent German police. Listening in to foreign radio stations was strictly prohibited. The press was severely censored, and broadcasting subjected to rigorous control; this made itself especially felt in the news bulletins, which became to a large extent trite reproductions of what the German propaganda ministry thought fit to present to its own people. At the same time, a great many items were inserted in radio programs, calculated to influence Dutch trend of thought. Great Britain is constantly represented as the embodiment of original sin, the country to which all evils, including the war, can be traced, and against which Germany is now crusading. The result of this campaign against the free opinion of the Dutch seems doubtful. The nation has for centuries been used to think for itself, the press has always been a free one, and the Dutch people, who, as members of a seafaring nation, have acquired some knowledge of the world, possess a gift of shrewd perspicacity which no propaganda can obliterate. The Dutch, unlike the Germans, are individualistic; the gregarious spirit, so characteristic of the Teuton race, is alien to them. Few, if any, of them have forgotten that the German invasion, which they know was at once universally condemned in all countries where thought and speech are free, and in particular by the Holy See, is at the bottom of their present sufferings. Moreover, they know too well how German propaganda methods work, not to be on their guard. Nevertheless, in this respect also their plight is a sad one. While realizing that what is broadcast over the radio under German dictate in their own language and what German censorship permits the familiar Dutch newspapers to print is often far from the truth, they are left to guess what the real truth is. This nation, accustomed for centuries past to look freely upon the world and to form its own opinion on the basis of what it has seen, now finds itself suddenly in the position of being told what to think and what to believe—a state of affairs so entirely at variance with Dutch customs and character that the result can not fail to be sullen scepticism and great uneasiness.

Once Holland was occupied, the German Fuehrer appointed Herr Seyss-Inquart, an Austrian politician whose share in the overthrow of Dr. Schuschnigg has not been forgotten, as Reich Commissioner for the Netherlands. His first act was a grave mistake, an outrage of all that is sacred to Dutch patriotic feeling. He thought fit to assume office in the ancient Hall of the Knights, the oldest building in The Hague, dating back to those far-off days of the early Middle Ages when the Counts of Holland ruled the region. That venerable building, the hallowed walls of which have witnessed so many historic scenes in the brilliant history of Holland, was the place where, once a year, the Queen opened Parliament in state. Now an emissary of Holland's conqueror summoned a number of Dutch officials there, together with a host of Nazi authorities, both civil and military, in order to assure them of the paternal interest he professed to take in safeguarding the country's well-being. "The Netherlands," so he said, "will, by offering all coöperation, assure their land and freedom for the future." The very word "freedom" in the mouth of Herr Hitler's proxy seems almost blasphemous, and it was remarkable, to use no stronger word, that he explained the term "coöperation" as meaning the subordination of all Dutch interests to the vital struggle of the German people. Speeches were also made by obsequious underlings—in that hall where a proud people used to raise its free voice—extolling the Fuehrer's good intentions towards Holland, and assuring that country, whose happiness, they said, was now at last assured, of the protection of the German armed forces, so necessary because the Dutch Government had been privy to the dark designs of British cunning. One can only feel deep aversion when listening to these dissonant notes. All elements of its national life, which the Dutch people had won for themselves, had jealously guarded through the ages, and to which it continued to be so deeply attached, were here represented as still present, whereas in reality all that was essential to a free nation had been taken away. Probably in order to mark German determination to ensure the happiness of Holland according to its own way, German music was played at the end of this distasteful ceremony.

It soon became apparent what Herr Seyss-Inquart's fine phrases meant. The Constitution of Holland was set aside: parliamentary institutions were suspended for an indefinite period. Instead of free enactments made by and with the consent of the people, decisions were imposed by the Reich Commissioner or by his police. The Dutch could but obey, and feel happy under so paternal and solicitous a rule. One of the oldest self-governing countries in the world suddenly found itself treated as if it were the home of eight million minors, incapable of looking after themselves. Humiliation and disgust must haunt the soul of every Dutchman.

Fear of Dutch loyalty to the House of Orange, coupled with the taste for oppression so characteristic of many Germans in their dealings with peoples they succeed in bringing under their rule, led them to commit a major blunder by prohibiting any demonstration of loyalty to the reigning House. With true German thoroughness, this prohibition was worked out in great detail. On birthdays of members of the royal family, the national flag must not be displayed, and no one is allowed to wear any national emblem, not even an orange-colored flower or—

so a proclamation of Seyss-Inquart said textually—a forget-me-not, or a white carnation as often worn by Prince Bernhard. Such is the petty mind of the would-be rulers of Europe. Let them display it—it can only damage their interests.

The Germans, for all their imposed rule, apparently realized that a people like that of Holland must be managed with at least some consideration if grave clashes were to be avoided. They accordingly practiced the policy of the iron hand in the velvet glove. As an "act of magnanimity" towards the people, whose only crime it was to have defended its liberties against aggression, Herr Hitler allowed all Dutch prisoners of war to be released and to return to their homes. A semblance of normal conditions was created by measures such as the reopening of museums and of theaters; but through it all runs the jarring note of an oppressive regime. The way in which the unemployment problem was tackled is a typical illustration. Extra workers had to be taken on or to be retained, whether they were needed or not, while thousands are gradually being put to work in Germany. Reconstruction work in devastated areas, especially in Rotterdam, was taken in hand so as to do away, as much as possible, with all evidence of the German conquest by force. Herr Seyss-Inquart, who loses no opportunity of attempting to ingratiate himself by assuring the Dutch of their Germanic origin, has made a tour of inspection through the country, which he rules not as it wishes to be ruled but as he sees fit. Germany is obviously attempting to gain some measure of good feeling on the part of her victims; but her chances of success seem slight. Even if she does not actually rule harshly, she has taken away too much of what is essential to the Dutch way of thinking to gain the nation's sympathy and support.

With the conquest of Holland, the Bolshevization of Europe has advanced another step. In many ways, Nazi doctrine and Nazi methods are related to those of Moscow. Both result in a general leveling down of the standard of living to a point below reasonable prosperity, and it yet remains to be seen whether Berlin and the Kremlin will succeed in raising it to any appreciable extent. In the Netherlands, this leveling down is very striking. Apart from the general rationing system, a very strict limit has been imposed on the possibility of drawing on bank accounts, so that inhabitants in the whole country are forced to live, at best, in very modest circumstances. Such are the blessings of Nazi rule.

It is difficult to form an impression of how these conditions will affect the spirit and the outlook of the Dutch nation. One thing, however, is certain: a race accustomed to free speech based on free thinking, cannot easily be forced to adopt methods which may be acceptable to Germans. For the time being, the country is ruled by force, and it realizes that open resistance would be less than futile. But this outward resignation should not be taken for inward submission. Just as the German loves authority from above, uniforms, and the spirit of the herd, so the Dutchman is fervently attached to autonomy, spontaneous order, and a happy compromise between the rights of the individual and the needs of the community. He hates coercion. And worse than avowed coercion is compulsion masquerading as liberty. Any such disguised form of constraint is doubly objectionable: it is insincere to all, and loathsome to those who, having once enjoyed the blessings of true liberty, at once recognize the adulterated variety for what it is. Enslavement parading as liberty is not therefore freedom.

Three hundred and sixty-five years ago, William the Silent founded the University of Leiden. The year before, the town had been besieged by the Spanish, but the population, in spite of famine and dire suffering, stubbornly held out until at last the enemy withdrew. As a reward, the Prince offered the town a choice between freedom from taxation for a number of years, or a university; the latter was chosen. On its seal are engraved the words, reminiscent forever of the origin of this venerable seat of learning: *Praesidium Libertatis*—"a stronghold of liberty." Its foundation day was celebrated, as it is every five years, in June of this year 1940. It was an even more than usually impressive ceremony, raised in these dark days to the significance of an act of faith. Professors and students assembled, not as usual in University Hall but in the old Church of St. Peter, dating back to the days of Spanish oppression, which has stood witness not only to more than one invasion of Holland, but also to as many resurrections from enslavement. The Rector of the University and its Chancellor, the Burgomaster of Leiden, in their speeches appealed to those present not to despair in the difficult times through which the country was passing, but to continue the great traditions of the University, steeped in a freedom of thought which knows no national frontiers in its pursuit of scientific truth. Then, breaking away from custom, the Chancellor asked his audience to sing "in the spirit of its founder" two verses of the Dutch national anthem, coeval with the University, and as the old church rang with the solemn words, exhorting the people to resist tyranny and to place their faith in God, the true spirit of the Netherlands could be heard for one brief, impressive moment. When the last sounds had faded away, that spirit became once more engulfed by an insidious, enemy-directed radio, by the vociferous propaganda of Dr. Goebbels' agents, by all the insincere clamor of the invader. But the short ceremony in the Leiden Church had shown the spiritual needs of the Dutch nation. For a few minutes, they had found a way of being themselves.

There seems little chance that, whatever attempts German propaganda may make to persuade the world that the Netherlands is now a happy, contented country, well satisfied with Herr Seyss-Inquart's benign rule, it will succeed in its purpose. The world knows that in Holland the tree of liberty is too deeply rooted to be eradicated overnight. It is not the destiny of this country to form part of any other country's "Lebensraum." Its geographical position is such that it cannot be completely within the political or economic sphere of Germany, of England, or of France. Here, in fact, lies one of the best guarantees for Holland's ultimate resurrection as an independent state. No power, however mighty, can in the long run successfully overrule the dictates of basic political facts. Has Germany understood this to be true? If she possesses real statesmen, not blinded by megalomania, she will admit this reality. So far, she has not done anything indicating blindness to these facts. She has not annexed the Netherlands, as she did in the case of Austria, the Czech inhabited portion of Czecho-Slovakia, Danzig, parts of Poland, and Eupen and Malmédy. Of course there is a possibility that, with regard to Holland, Germany is biding the ultimate outcome of the war, and meanwhile wishes to keep her hands free. Let us hope that, whatever that outcome may be, statesmanlike insight will preside over the decisions which will then have to be taken. If that hope is realized, Holland will be set free. If not, there will be no real peace in Western Europe until it is.

It is realized the world over, that the occupation of Holland is but one element in the war against a political ideology based on force, in which the individual counts for nothing. As such, the ultimate fate of the Netherlands has a significance far beyond its narrow frontiers. It would be a sad loss to the world if this country, where once stood

the cradle of that free thought which has so profoundly
stimulated the happiness of other nations and races, were
to remain subjugated against the will of its inhabitants,
who still have a contribution to make to the common fund
of human knowledge and well-being.

Meanwhile, the struggle between spiritual liberty and
enslavement of the soul goes on. France has been overpowered, but the other Allied countries, and among them
Holland, continue the fight, headed by the British Empire. They have free access to by far the greater part of
the world's material resources. The industrial power of
the United States of America is of the greatest importance
in enabling them still to hold their banner high. Their
resources in man power have not been drawn upon to
nearly the same extent as those of Germany, where in
addition, food, oil products, and many other commodities
necessary for a successful prosecution of war are becoming increasingly scarce.

There was a time, only a few years ago, when Britain's
first defenses were said to be on the Rhine. Now, the defenses of the Netherlands are on Britain's shores. And this
admirable British island fortress holds! Not only does it
hold, but it strikes back with ever harder blows, in con-
fident anticipation of victory.

Against this background, the Government of the Netherlands carries on its work in London. As soon as its
members had all arrived there, they at once set to work
to keep the machinery of Government going. They were

joined by a number of civil servants and experts, who had
either been able to escape or had found their way to London from places abroad where they happened to be on
some official mission when war broke out. Scores of matters in connection with the war asked for immediate attention. The Foreign Ministry, the Ministry of Defense
and the Ministry for the Colonies are working under high
pressure. The diplomatic and consular services of the
Netherlands continue to function as usual, keeping in constant touch with headquarters, and are more than ever
out to further the interests of the Dutch Colonies. Of special concern were Dutch rights and interests in other
countries, as it was to be foreseen that Germany would
leave nothing undone, acting either directly or through
intermediaries, to lay hands on Dutch assets in neutral
countries, especially in the Western Hemisphere. Everything possible was done to frustrate attempts in that direction. Towards spring, when the military situation in
Western Europe grew more tense, the Dutch Government had begun taking all possible measures to be ready
in case the country were attacked. The possibility was
created of transferring the seat of Dutch companies and
corporations to Netherlands overseas territories, thereby
removing them further from the grasp of an occupying
power. Legislation was prepared to prevent trading with
the enemy in the East Indies, in Surinam and in Curaçao,
with the result that the necessary regulations could be enforced there from the first day of the invasion. Provisions

were also made to insure that the foreign services of the Netherlands would never stop functioning owing to lack of funds. It may be said that little had been left to chance, but it stands to reason that not everything could be done before it was known that Germany was the invader.

Thus, for instance, the legal position of Dutch assets abroad was made secure only after the Government arrived in London. The decision then taken deserves special mention because of its far-reaching character in preventing economic interests of Dutch citizens abroad from falling into German hands. A Royal Decree was issued, vesting in the State of the Netherlands, represented by its legitimate Government, the ownership of all property and financial claims abroad, belonging to individuals and institutions established in the Kingdom of the Netherlands. The State is only allowed to exercise this right of ownership in order to safeguard the interests thus taken over, which are to be returned to the original owners three months after the present state of emergency will have ceased to exist. The requisite measures were taken to implement this decree, instituting custodians where necessary and providing for all other problems in connection with this typical instance of emergency legislation.

When war broke out, about two-thirds of the very considerable quantity of gold belonging to the State of the Netherlands and to the Netherlands Bank was in safe places overseas, chiefly in the United States of America. Immediately upon the German invasion, all possible measures were successfully taken to evacuate whatever gold still remained in the country. Actuated by spitefulness, the German propaganda organization used this theme in an effort to stir up feeling amongst the Dutch nation against the Government, whose members, so Dr. Goebbels' services said, had absconded with the country's gold. The Foreign Minister was even said to have left the country after stuffing his pockets at the last moment with the "State diamonds"—precious stones existing only in the fervid imagination of those who invented this romantic story, which they apparently hoped would have some cheap popular appeal.

A subject to which the Government devoted much care and attention was the problem of the Dutch refugees who, driven from their homes in Holland, had fled first to Belgium and, when that unfortunate country had also been occupied by the enemy, drifted farther and farther into France, pursued by the invader. Others, although far less numerous, had managed in some way or another to escape to the British Isles where, it should be gratefully recalled, as in France and later in Spain and Portugal much was done for their welfare. The forty thousand hapless fugitives in France presented a difficult problem. Under the supervision of a Government Commissioner for refugees residing in London, a sub-Commissioner was sent to France and later to Spain, to minister to the needs of these wretched people. In this way much human suffering was alleviated, if not prevented.

With the help of the French, and later with the British authorities, it was arranged from the outset that radio broadcasts were sent out from Paris, and subsequently from London, in the Dutch language, in an effort to acquaint the Dutch population with the true state of world affairs. It was felt that these broadcasts would not fail to have a heartening effect on a people left to live on their own moral stamina, and constantly showered with German propaganda. It was with this in mind that, on Prince Bernhard's birthday, June 29th, on which day the Germans had "verboten" the display of the Dutch flag, the Minister for the Interior made a stirring broadcast from London to the Dutch people, voicing the sentiments that were theirs on that day to which they could give no expression themselves.

Although in Holland the national flag is at present overshadowed by the swastika banner, that flag flies freely in the overseas territories. There, the news of the invasion was received with great consternation. The white inhabitants thought of their relatives in the home country, anxiously wondering what the outcome would be and filled with helpless fury at being so far away; the native population, more and more alive to the leniency and progressive spirit of Dutch rule suddenly realized, as they had never done before, that for them, too, much was at stake. The news of the enemy's rapid advance came as a surprise and a great shock: so far from the actual scene of operations, it was more difficult than in Europe to realize by what

novel enemy devices and trickery Dutch resistance, which
had been so carefully prepared, had been so rapidly un-
dermined. Soon, however, these feelings of amazement
gave way to those of deep loyalty to Queen and Government and of compassion for the mother country, not
only throughout the white population, but also, to an
extent never witnessed before, throughout the native population as well.

A wave of loyal feeling swept over the colonies; it had
to manifest itself in some tangible form. Thousands vol-
unteered for the Dutch services. Thousands took part in
patriotic demonstrations and, above all, everybody contributed towards the fund, bearing the Queen's name,
which was at once instituted for the relief of the stricken
home country. Nobody even stopped to think whether
it would be possible to bring relief, while Holland was
writhing under German occupation. They had to find
some outlet for their loyalty by action, and the impulse
of their generosity made them act at once. Large dona-
tions were received, but welcome though they were, it is
the spirit that prompted the innumerable small gifts which
is so significant. Most of these came from people who had
little, if anything, to spare, native as well as white. Among
the most moving of these truly voluntary contributions
were the wedding rings of a number of minor civil servants. Never has there been more overwhelming evidence
of the strength of the bonds uniting the far-flung parts
of the Dutch Empire.

In the overseas colonies, order and security continue to prevail. The shock caused by the invasion of the mother country had no repercussion in the administration of these territories, nor was their international status in any way impaired. Not that this status left others indifferent. On the contrary, the United States, Great Britain, and Japan all expressed their profound interest in the maintenance of the *status quo* of the Dutch East Indies, which was thereby once more proclaimed to be a matter of universal concern. All interested governments realize that the Dutch are capable of insuring, as they have done for more than three centuries, the administration and the welfare of their Indian Empire, at the same time opening their resources to all the world. To that rule there is only one exception: the enemy is to be denied access to these important markets. But otherwise, Japan and the United States of America no less than the Allies, can obtain in the Indian archipelago all they require, so long as there is plenty for everybody.

What remained of the Dutch army, after the heavy losses it suffered during the five days of armed resistance, was disbanded by the Germans. About two thousand men were able to escape, in various ways and in many cases by long circuitous routes, to England. There they have been equipped once more, to be ready for future service. The Royal Navy, by far the greater part of which is always stationed overseas, is virtually intact, although a few valuable units were lost during the battle. What vessels, officers, and men are in Europe, now take an active part in Allied naval operations against Germany, operations in which our excellent submarines play a conspicuous part. In the East and West Indies, the bulk of the Dutch Fleet guards the safety of these colonies, together with powerful land and air forces, the latter equipped with modern American airplanes in no inconsiderable numbers. The Dutch mercantile marine, which ranks among the largest in the world, and by far the greater part of which was prevented from falling into enemy hands, forms another important contribution to the successful prosecution of war. As so often in the course of history, these elements once more demonstrate that, whatever fate may temporarily overtake the Netherlands in Europe, the spirit of Holland, to whose seafaring traditions true air-mindedness has of late been added, is alive and remains undaunted.

German ideologists, with their strange ways of abstruse reasoning, may think that the Low Countries can be coaxed or driven into accepting a place of dependence in the Third Reich. They are wrong, as they have always been wrong because, although they may understand German ways of thinking, they do not understand human nature. A nation which, for centuries, has been used to free institutions, never loses the taste of them—not in one, not in two, not in three generations. And so long as the true history of the Netherlands is whispered from ear to ear lest the Gestapo should hear it, the foundations are there on which, one glorious day, the independent State of the Netherlands will once again take its place among the free nations of the world. That no tyrant, no usurper can prevent.

The Germans can try to cajole the people of the Netherlands, or they can try to terrorize them. They can starve them to the extent that they starve their own civilians the better to feed their military forces, or they can starve them more severely. They can treat the people of Holland, who have never done them any harm, in a decent manner, or they can resort to brutality and plunder. But, whatever they do, they can not convince their victims that it was not Germany who attacked them in their sleep; that it is not Germany who, in that country where good food was plentiful, causes them to be ill-fed; that it is not Germany's fault when the heart of the young mother is wrung with despair, seeing that her baby is deprived of proper nourishment and clothing; that Germany is not to blame when trade languishes, when the country's resources are rapidly dwindling, when poverty and misery begin to stare around every corner in that country which, left alone, was happy and prosperous; when there is nothing to be bought in the shops because Germans have laid hands on everything since the first moment of the occupation; when there is nothing but gloom, and suspicion, and ill-concealed hatred, and the ruins of Rotterdam, raising their gaping wounds to heaven.

But no—there is something else. There is the keen sense

that the Netherlands must become a free country again. Its people cannot be permanently enslaved, they will not be stifled, they cannot breathe in that sullen, oppressive atmosphere. As soon as the chance comes, the people of the Netherlands will free themselves, just as they freed themselves in the days of Spanish tyranny, or when, in 1672, all Europe seemed to turn against them; or after Napoleon's star had fallen. Against them, all despots have played a losing game. That they know. Never was the country's history a more abundant source of inspiration, a more treasured possession, a richer fund of comfort and of strength.

Holland bides its hour: sooner or later, it knows that hour will strike.

Index